Also by Ronald Hirsch

The Self in No Self: Buddhist Heresies and Other Lessons of a Buddhist Life

Making Your Way in Life as a Buddhist: A Practical Guide

Raising a Happy Child: A Practical Guide

We STILL Hold These Truths: Preserving the Heart of American Democracy for the 21st Century

Scratching the Itch

Getting to the Root of Our Suffering

Ronald Hanh Niêm Hirsch

ThePracticalBuddhist.com Publishing

Published 2012 by ThePracticalBuddhist.com Publishing, Stuyvesant, NY 12173. U.S. © 2012 Ronald L. Hirsch. All rights reserved.

No part of this publication may be reproduced, stored in a retrieval system, or transmitted in any form or by any means, electronic, mechanical, recording or otherwise, without the prior written permission of Ronald L. Hirsch

ISBN 978-0-9883290-4-1 (softcover), 978-0-9883290-5-8 (eBook)

To the Ven. Huyen Te and Ven. Thai Tue,
who imparted clear and insightful teaching
into the heart of the Buddha dharma,
revealing the path to end suffering.

TABLE OF CONTENTS

Preface	1
1 Only You Can Do It	5
2 First Things First - Building a Platform of Serenity	7
I Believe – The Importance of Faith	9
Aware Breath = Instant Samadhi	12
The Power of Smiling Mindfully	15
Take Joy in Each Moment, in Everything You Do	18
Accepting Ourselves –	
Cultivating a Compassionate Heart	21
Accepting Life	26
Staying Grounded	32
3 Why Do We Crave? – The Root of All Suffering	41
4 Discovering the Emptiness of Thought	49
5 Practicing the Six Paramitas	59
6 Surrendering the Ego and Finding Freedom	85

Preface

When Zen Master Bankei was a young monk and seeking instruction, he traveled to many temples to receive teaching from learned and respected monks. Yet each time he was left wanting. What he had been taught did not take him further along the path. He was as far from enlightenment as he had been before.

After a grueling period of aestheticism almost killed him and realizing that the mortification of his body had brought him no further towards enlightenment, much like the Buddha, he suddenly found his truth in the Unborn. Afterwards, when he went to talk with an elder Zen monk about this and receive instruction, the following dialogue ensued.

> "All that you and everyone else here has said to me is very true. It's not that I don't agree with it. Only, somehow or other, the feeling I get is that of scratching an itchy foot with my shoe on. It's not getting to the itch. The teachings don't strike home to the center, to the real marrow,"[1]

I had been walking the Buddhist path for a number of years and had also not made much progress. I had gone to temple, heard innumerable dharma talks, and meditated daily, but although I received much good teaching and learned much, I was not really any further along the path. I experienced greater calm in my life and I had built a platform of serenity based on gratefulness and acceptance,

---

[1] Norman Waddell, *The Unborn: The Life and Teachings of Zen Master Bankei*, North Point Press, 1984, p.52

but the suffering that was at the core of my ego had not been eased.

Then I had the good fortune to have a new teacher come into my life, the Vietnamese Zen monk, Ven. Huyen Te. Huyen Te was transformative, unlike any teacher that I had experienced previously. He had no use for teaching that did not go to the heart of Buddhist practice. He wanted to make those insights, that wisdom, available to us all. Huyen Te knew that only through our understanding and ultimately internalizing the central insights of Buddhism could we change the paradigms that control our lives and are the cause of our suffering.

And he knew that the path was difficult because it meant changing the way in which we viewed ourselves and the world around us. It required discipline. And so he pushed us in every way. Over the course of a few months, Huyen Te increased our sitting time to 1 hour 15 minutes. It was difficult and initially painful, but taking us out of our comfort zone and showing us what was possible was an integral part of his teaching.

The dharma talks were rigorous. Week after week, approaching the same subject matter in different ways, he pounded home the two most essential truths of Buddhism ... that our perceptions are illusory and that all things are impermanent and changeable.

After months of teaching and a deepening of my practice, I had made much progress and yet the core issues that formed my samsara[2] remained impervious. Then one day during a dharma talk, Huyen Te said that we had come far but we were still standing on the precipice. We were not able to jump because our ego was still in control and we feared an ego-free unknown. He said that the choice was ours, we had only to surrender our ego to our true Buddha nature. It was as straight forward as that.

---

[2] Samsara is the endless cycle of suffering caused by our ego-driven unskillful actions and emotions/reactions.

It is now many years since I first heard Huyen Te say we had but to surrender our ego to our true Buddha nature; that the choice was ours. After much practice and turning inward, I did finally surrender my ego to my true Buddha nature, turning my will and my life over to my true Buddha nature, yet I cannot say that it never rears its head, that it has no influence. Enlightenment for most of us is an incremental path; indeed, if I ever reach that state, I don't know how I would know it. But I am observing now through different eyes and when it whispers in my ear, I am fully aware and mindful. My suffering has ceased.

I have benefited greatly from Huyen Te's teaching that "scratched the itch." This book seeks to take that teaching ... which I referenced in a previous book, *The Self in No Self: Buddhist Heresies and Other Lessons of a Buddhist Life* ... and expound upon it, expanding it, in light of my personal practical experience of walking the path in the hope of helping others in their effort to end their suffering.

While enlightenment may not be a very practical goal for most of us walking the Buddhist path, attaining a state in our practice that is close to enlightenment[3] is a goal that every person committed to the path can attain with the necessary belief in the teachings of the Buddha and a disciplined practice.

---

[3] In classic Buddhist teaching, there are four stages of enlightenment ... the stream-enterer, the once-returner, the non-returner, and the arahant, the last of which is referred to as fully enlightened. Each stage is defined by how many fetters ... the chains that cause samsara, such as self/ego, doubt, ill will, greed, lust ... one has abandoned.

Chapter 1
Only You Can Do It

Buddhism is not a religion in which one prays to God or some external higher power to right ones life, to release ones burdens, or to end ones suffering.[4] The teaching of Buddhism is that it is left to ourselves to transform our lives. We are our own higher power, or better put, our own true Buddha nature is our higher power.

Many people are confused by the statues of the Buddha and bodhisatvas that one finds on the alters of temples. They are confused by the practice of prostrating oneself before the Buddha statue. They think of the statues and the prostrations in the context of the religions they were brought up in ... namely that one is praying to the Buddha for deliverance.

But they have a basic misunderstanding. The statues of the Buddha and bodhisattvas are there for symbolic and inspirational purposes. They have no other meaning; they are not stand-ins for the Buddha. When we prostrate ourselves before the Buddha, it is out of respect to the teachings of the Buddha and to our own true Buddha nature. It is a physical manifestation of submitting our ego to our true Buddha nature. We do not prostrate ourselves to ask the Buddha for anything.

The centrality of ones responsibility for oneself can also be seen in the often-found statement by Buddhist teachers that they are not seeking to set up yet another

---

[4] Indeed, Buddhism is not a religion at all in the normal sense of the word; it is instead a way of life. In addition to not praying to the Buddha for deliverance, there is no creation story in Buddhism, which is a standard feature of other religions.

structure, a system of authority, for people to follow that would only create yet another source of conflict for them. Instead they are merely trying to point the way for each person to find their own path to freedom.

The wisdom is there for each person to find, but only the individual can come to an understanding and realization of that wisdom. And only through such understanding and realization can we be free of suffering.

And so, it is left for you to decide. You are venturing on a great journey of the spirit that has the potential to free your mind, body, and soul and bring you peace and happiness. Are you ready to make the commitment to follow the path, to practice with discipline, and have the faith and infinite patience that will be necessary for you as you walk the path?

You are attempting to change the paradigms of your life, to free yourself from the learned experience and habits of a lifetime. This is not an easy task you have set for yourself, but it is without any question a practical task so long as you have the necessary belief in the teachings of the Buddha and a commitment to a disciplined practice.

I wish you well.

Chapter 2
First Things First - Building a Platform of Serenity

Serenity. What a completely foreign concept this was to me. How can anyone be serene unless they're a saint? All I'd known in my life was constant inner turmoil, certainly since I was a young child. And in looking around at my peers and family, and at the images of the larger culture, I didn't see anyone who was serene. My parents may have been in love and friends laughed and relaxed, but that's not serenity. Everyone was beset with problems that disturbed them. Even in the idealistic sitcoms of the 50s, whether it was the Beaver, or Ozzie and Harriet, or Lucy ... everyone's lives were filled with conflict and confusion. Yet I knew in my gut that serenity and a life free of suffering was a rational, reasonable goal. The question was not whether, but how?

. . . .

I had been a practicing Buddhist for several years, but my practice was not progressing. My life was definitely calmer, but my mind was not quiet, even when sitting on my cushion. I had been going to temple, but the teaching was not challenging and didn't move me forward on the path.

What I had learned about the basics of Buddhist philosophy through reading, however, motivated me to go deeper with my practice. It all made sense to me, and yet it was so foreign to my experience and our culture that I knew making progress would not be easy.

Just as space explorers need to go to an orbiting platform before venturing into deep space, I felt I needed to create a platform of serenity upon which to build further explorations of my mind.

I had thought that serenity would come as a natural product of meditation. But although I meditated daily, it didn't seem to increase my serenity.

For meditation to "work", I realized that not only is it important to create a physical atmosphere that is calm, it is important to have a psyche that, if not abidingly calm, at least is not in constant turmoil. Otherwise, try as I may to focus on my breathing during meditation, my mind would be bombarded with thoughts of the unfinished business of my life; my ego would not give me much rest. I was calm during meditation, but I did not experience much peace.

And so I slowly built a platform of serenity based on the steps outlined in the following sections. It is a practical, realizable approach. It speaks to the goal of attaining a serenity that enables one to begin experiencing peace, happiness, and hope in the present by beginning to lift obstructions and frustration from your mind and soul ... a serenity we need to make skillful decisions in our lives and the peace necessary for the deeper exploration of our mind.[5]

This is not the answer. This is not yet the teaching that scratches the itch. But it will put you in a position to access that teaching, attain a deeper understanding of the truths of the Buddha dharma and the workings of your mind.

---

[5] This material appeared in essentially the same form in my previously published book, *The Self in No Self: Buddhist Heresies and Other Lessons of a Buddhist Life*. I repeat it here as I did in my book, *Making Your Way in Life as a Buddhist*, because it is an essential first step for most of us in any attempt to end our suffering and lead a Buddhist life.

I BELIEVE – THE IMPORTANCE OF FAITH

Because following the Buddhist path means going against the grain of almost everything in our learned experience, everything our ego and our culture tells us, I quickly found that it is not a walk in the park. It requires commitment, discipline and patience. And to be able to apply those three practices in the face of the obstacles and struggles we face daily requires deep faith … faith in the teachings of the Buddha.

For many people, "faith" is a loaded word from their religious upbringing. But faith, or belief, in the Buddha dharma is qualitatively different from the faith that is sought in most religious contexts. Religious faith often requires belief in something that flies in the face of reason. Whether it's a belief in God, or belief in the virgin birth and resurrection of Jesus, or the Trinity, or the countless miracles … all of these things require what's often called a "leap of faith" or sometimes "blind faith."

In Buddhism, the situation is different. In Buddhism there is no God; there is no creation story … things just are. When most of us read a Buddhist text or listen to a good dharma talk, we respond by saying, "Of course, that makes such perfect sense. I can relate that so well to what I've experienced." In general, our intellect is on board rather quickly with our following the Buddhist path.

For Buddhists, it is the ego, our habit energy, that must be successfully countered if we are to make progress on the path. When the core of my ego screamed at me, "I want!" as I worked to be grateful for the wonderful things in my life or accept my life as it is now, it was only my deep faith in the teachings of the Buddha that provided me with the strength to say to my ego, "no."

That faith has two main components. The first is faith that the path provided by the Buddha dharma will end our suffering … provided that we have the strength to follow it.

That sounds like it should be simple. That is, after all, why we are Buddhists. Yes, there are many other features of Buddhism that make it attractive to us, but it is the desire to end our suffering that keeps us persevering.

And yet having deep faith in our chosen path is not simple. That is because at this stage of our practice we are still primarily creatures of the ego, of feelings, of perceptions; our true Buddha nature, our unborn mind is virtually a stranger to us. And the sum of our learned experience in the form of our ego will throw every thing it can at us to subvert us from the path. Only by staying focused on my faith in the teachings was I able to withstand this sometimes seemingly relentless pressure.

The other main component is faith in our own true Buddha nature. While this concept doesn't fly in the face of reason, it doesn't easily respond to the intellect either.

There are many rationale that compromise our belief in our true Buddha nature. One is, if we were born with our true Buddha nature and it's still there, why has it allowed us to suffer so? Why doesn't it show itself more clearly, even when we are searching for it? We often find this hard to grasp.

For those brought up in the Christian faith, another problem is the concept of original sin ... the exact opposite of the Buddhist belief. If you had the concept of being born a sinner drummed into your head in church during your formative years, it is understandable that the concept of being born perfect would be a challenging, albeit a welcomed, one.

Finally, because for most of us our true Buddha nature has been buried under the many layers of learned experience that form our ego, the fact that it is not visible to us, that we can't touch it somehow, is an obstacle to our belief. We have to take it as a matter of faith, until we are sufficiently aware that we begin to see glimpses of our true Buddha nature revealed to us. This happens when we begin observing without the intervention of thought[6] and we become aware of the discrepancy between what our ego is whispering in our ear about something and what our true Buddha nature is telling us.

Sometimes, visualization can be an important aid in understanding or projecting something. I had been trying for some time while meditating to somehow connect with my true Buddha nature, to visualize this non-physical thing, to no avail. Then one day, as I was meditating, I suddenly saw before me smiling, laughing images of me as a toddler. I knew immediately that there was my true Buddha nature, taking joy in the moment for no particular reason, full of love, an innocent in the world unburdened by learned experience. Not uncoincidently I'm sure, I had within the previous few months received from my mother both my baby book and an album of photos of me as a baby and toddler!

But at bottom, if we believe in the teachings of the Buddha, then we believe that each of us is born with our true Buddha nature intact and that it remains a part of us forever … the one thing that is not impermanent and changeable.

Armed by our faith, there will be a counterforce within us whenever our ego tries to get us to give up the path or question it.

---

[6] As will be discussed later on, it is not that one doesn't have thoughts, but that one doesn't attach to them or engage them, and therefore they do not intervene in our observations.

AWARE BREATH = INSTANT SAMADHI

It's all fine and well being in a calm, peaceful state when one is meditating, sitting on ones cushion, but what happens while we're going through the rest of the day? Remaining in that state while encountering all the stressors of everyday life seemed an impossible challenge to me. Meditation became a time-bound refuge, not an every-moment lifestyle.

The usual advice regarding this problem is to be mindful throughout the day, to observe, to be aware. Unfortunately for most of us, mindfulness always seems to come after the event, after we have reacted to something in a decidedly unmindful way. This makes for a teachable moment, but does not help us much in the process of establishing a mindful state throughout the day.

The problem is one of focus. When we sit on our cushion to meditate, we learn from the outset to focus on our breathing ... breathing in, breathing out ... not to cut out what is happening around us or the thoughts that flow through our minds, but just to be aware of those things while focusing on our breath. This allows us to be mindful. But when we are not sitting, meditating, our minds are focused on all the various things happening around us.

One day while I was sitting, I practiced breathing in a way suggested by an article I had recently read ... I felt my breath come in as I expanded my diaphragm, rise up through my lungs, expand my upper back muscles, and then descend again to my diaphragm when I exhaled. As I practiced this method of breathing, and observed it, the image came to me that my breath was like a wave washing gently over my body. And just as waves cleanse the sand, so too my breath ... the breath of life ... was cleansing my body and soul.

I understood then that focusing on our breathing while meditating is not just a tool to help us stay focused; the awareness of breathing in and out is the basic building block of meditation. I realized that with each *aware* breath, regardless whether we are sitting on our cushion meditating or out and about, we are mindful, evils are extinguished, karma is purified, and obstructions dissolved.

But the question then became, how to achieve that awareness when I'm not sitting. When we sit to meditate, we are doing something purposeful that makes it easy … well, easier … to focus on our breathing. What we need to do, at least in the beginning, is to do something similarly purposeful at various points throughout the day.

The first step is to purposefully just stop whatever you're doing, mentally and physically, for a moment or a few. Because if you don't stop you can't take the next step and focus on your spirituality.

In Korean Zen, there are various chants/exercises based on the word, ma-um, which means, "mind." One of the exercises is, "breathing in we say 'ma,' which relaxes the body, breathing out we say 'um,' which relaxes the mind." This was something I could do periodically throughout the day, I thought.

And what I've found is that after doing the exercise (3 times in succession), I not only am aware of my breath, but I am instantly in the relaxed peaceful state that I experience when sitting on my cushion meditating. I may remain in that state, focused on my breathing, for as few as a few breaths or as long as several minutes, depending on what's going on around me.

Another technique that has worked for me is just saying the mantra, "Breathing in, I am aware that I am breathing in. Breathing out, I am aware that I am breathing out." Again, saying this 3 times in succession has brought me to a quiet, meditative state.

Once you are in a meditative state, and thus centered, observe whether you are or, more importantly, have been just prior to your entering this meditative state, in a state of equanimity, whether you feel compassion for yourself and others, whether you have been observing ... that is *not* engaging ... your feelings, whether you are accepting of yourself and the world around you.

If the answer to any of these queries is, "no," then if the situation allows, continue to meditate to regain the state of equanimity. If the situation does not allow continued meditation, at least you will be aware that you are not in a state of equanimity and be mindful of your actions and thoughts.

It may not sound like much, but these on-the-feet mini-meditations have enabled me to be more mindful throughout the day. Try it ... you'll like it.

THE POWER OF SMILING MINDFULLY

Most of us are frustrated or at least concerned about many aspects of our lives, both large and small. So when we hear or read that the teaching of Buddhism says to accept things as being the way they are because it's just the way it is, we have a problem with that teaching. I certainly pushed back against it initially because I did not *want* to accept things as being the way they are ... even for a moment. I may have said, "I accept," but I didn't really accept.

On the one hand, I had approached Buddhism because I wanted to end my suffering, but on the other hand I really didn't want to do what I had to do to end that suffering. I feared the unknown ... if I accepted things as they are, then how would I pursue the rest of my life?[7]

While nothing can take the place of meditation in removing these obstructions and bringing us closer to acceptance, there is a shortcut to at least lessen the frustration and thereby ease that barrier ... smiling mindfully.

As you go through the day, try to be aware of your facial expression. If you're like me, you'll find that in general your facial muscles are either frowning or in a serious repose. This is our usual state when we're alone with our thoughts as opposed to being engaged in conversation with others or being entertained.

I regret that it was only after years of Buddhist practice and experiencing in general a state of peace and contentment that I became aware one day that most of the time my facial muscles were tense. And as I observed my tense facial muscles, I became aware that this tenseness created a state of non-joy that was at odds with the peace and contentment that I was otherwise experiencing.

---

[7] For more on this, see the section, "The Desire That Is Right Desire," in my book, *The Self in No Self: Buddhist Heresies and Other Lessons of a Buddhist Life*.

Purposefully, I brought a smile to my face and found that this in turn brought an immediate uplift to my spirits. Just releasing the facial tension made me feel lighter and filled with happiness. This is what Thich Nhat Hanh calls "mouth yoga." But I found that the smile and its impact were fleeting because it was mechanical and I was quickly distracted.

Then one day while meditating, I realized that if I were able to be aware every moment of the wonderful things in my life right then at each moment, without attaching, I would smile mindfully and naturally every moment. Even if I was focused on some concern of mine, I would at the same time be mindful of the things that brought joy to my life.

Well, every moment was perhaps too much to expect at the start. But every moment I was aware of my breath, I would say to myself, "I am grateful for all the wonderful things in my life right now at this moment," and as those things came to mind I could feel myself smiling. As time passed, I observed that my awareness of the good things in my life began to permeate my day and I smiled more, not just when I was aware of my breath.

But this experience raised a question in my mind ... if I was generally in a state of peace and contentment, then why was the default status of my face a frown or serious expression?

Generally we frown for various reasons ... our culture is so focused on wanting what we don't have (not necessarily something material) and on proving ourselves through competition, we are so attached to the past and obsessed with the future, and the problems of the world around us are so vexing that most of us are in an almost constant state of some degree of frustration or concern, whether consciously or not. If we are frustrated, we are not happy, and that agitation shows in our facial expression.

Was my frowning a sign of the deep underlying

frustration and insecurity in my gut that my practice had not yet touched? Were the troubles of the world and especially U.S. politics so overburdening? As a Buddhist I derive joy from the happiness of others, but the corollary is also true, I derive sadness from the pain of others.

Or was this default position merely a product of decades of negative muscle training brought about by my samsara-filled life? I know from my baby photos and family anecdotes that before I was burdened by my ego and learned experience I always had a smile on my face. My father called me his "sunshine."

My hunch was "all of the above." Of course this practice of smiling mindfully did not change my underlying condition or the reality of the world with its problems. But it did provide me with a renewed focus on the positive in my life and increased my experience of joy and happiness.

The strengthening of this positive perspective brought me back to basics, opening me up to more fully accepting things as being the way they are, releasing obstructions, and going deep within myself in meditation. By doing so, it gave me more energy to tackle the challenges of life with Right view, free of illusion.

TAKE JOY IN EACH MOMENT, IN EVERYTHING YOU DO

A monk once said to me, "Take joy, Ron, in each moment, in everything you do."

In our culture, we are programmed to seek out things to do that will be fun. Whether it's going out and buying something, going to some cultural event, taking a trip, or countless other options. The point is, to do something other than what we are currently doing, something that is not required of us or part of our daily routine.

We always want something different, something new, to stimulate us. The result is that we take no joy in the everyday aspects of our lives. How sad when right before our eyes, every moment of every day, there is something to take joy in and value. It's all a matter of perspective.

For years I paid no attention to the monk's simple teaching and my life was very unsettled despite a disciplined practice of daily meditation and reading. Then one day while I was meditating, this teaching came to mind and I let it sit there while I observed it and took its measure. It was one of those "eureka" moments. I resolved from that day onward, at first purposefully, to do as the monk had taught.

To take joy in each moment, one must first be present in the moment. If your thinking about this and that ... what you're going to be doing later in the day, how some problem will resolve itself, whatever ... then you can't take joy in the moment because that requires the focus of being present. There's a time for those thoughts, but it's not when you're getting dressed or doing laundry; it's when you sit down purposefully to think about those things because you need to be present for those thoughts as well.

I remember that first day well. Purposefully, I was present in each moment, something that was surprisingly rare for me despite my years of practice and disciplined daily meditation; such is the power of our mind. Everything I did, from the most mundane tasks of washing and drying the dishes or feeling the soft material of a knit top as I pulled it on to more mentally challenging tasks such as reading to just looking out and seeing the wind play with the grasses, tossing their seed heads this way and that in an undulating ballet ... I literally took joy in every moment, in everything I did.

Whether you live in the country or the city, are rich or poor, are educated or not, this practice is available to all. When you are doing a task, even a very repetitive or menial one, or just being you have a choice whether to be bored or take joy.

Be aware of the motions of your body or the actions of your mind in accomplishing that task and strive to do the best you can in accomplishing it. Do it purposefully, not carelessly; give it thought, give it structure, give it dignity. Be aware of the layers of texture and the countless minute miracles of nature or science that are involved in your being able to accomplish the task well or just in your being alive. No task is mindless; no moment is without wonder and dignity.

When you are out and about, whether walking down a crowded city street or walking through a country meadow, let all your senses be alive with the experience, free of thought. Let's say you're walking in the city. You have a choice whether to focus on the dirt and noise and traffic and find it depressing, or feel the energy, the diversity of people, the amazing fact that somehow all of this works in unison. Likewise if you're walking in the country on a very hot summer day, you have the choice to focus on how uncomfortable you feel because of the heat or you can focus on the hugely varied texture and miracle of nature that is available to your senses.

In a way, this practice can be thought of as a further step in the practice of smiling mindfully. When we begin that practice and think of the wonderful things in our life, we typically think of larger, more significant things that play a major role in our lives. In this practice, we realize that all the minutiae of our lives are full of wonder and available to take joy in; we are aware of the dignity of our lives. And being present provides the access, the door to experiencing that joy and dignity.

ACCEPTING OURSELVES – CULTIVATING A COMPASSIONATE HEART

For years I wandered through my life frustrated. It didn't matter whether I was doing something I enjoyed or whether I was keeping up with what was happening in the world. What I enjoyed awakened cravings that left me anxious and frustrated. What disturbed me in the world left me feeling angry and agitated. And of course not having what I waned left me frustrated and angry. The problem was that I was approaching everything in my life from a place that lacked equanimity.

If we want to be in this world and not be agitated by all the terrible things that are happening, if we want to do the things we enjoy and give our life purpose without awakening cravings and frustration, if we want to feel at peace and contentment, there is one clear answer ... acceptance. Until I truly accepted myself and my life as it was right then and accepted the world as it was right then, I was constantly subject to the suffering, the agony, caused by craving, frustration, and anger.

The first step is to accept *ourselves* ... to have compassion for ourselves and love ourselves unconditionally. For myself, as for so many people, learning to love myself unconditionally and have compassion for myself was a real challenge.

Why is it so hard for us to have compassion for ourselves? One would think that compassion would be a significant coping mechanism. But our ego, while supportive of every manner of rationalization to justify our actions or our failure to act, does not allow us to feel compassion for ourselves because that would undermine the power of the learned labels that it ruthlessly applies to us.

"Wait," you say, "I have felt pity towards myself or sorrow at my condition." But pity and sorrow are not compassion, at least not in the Buddhist sense. Because pity and sorrow do not negate the underlying condition as perceived by our ego. It does not change the perception that we are bad or a failure or whatever.

"Well, what about all the people out there with huge egos? Are you saying they don't love themselves?" They may love themselves, but certainly not unconditionally and they don't have compassion for themselves. People with huge egos have been shown to be at bottom very insecure people. The huge ego is a façade that hides their insecurity.

For a Buddhist, the origin of compassion is love, whether for oneself or others. It is selfless and unconditional. When compassion flows from unconditional love, we do not judge ourselves anymore. We accept ourselves for what we are ... without labels.

So how do we cultivate unconditional love and compassion while still in the throes of our ego? The answer comes in two parts ... one organic, one intellectual.

Before we know our true Buddha nature, before we understand the illusory nature of all perceptions, before we have freed ourselves from the past and the future, we understand samsara.

We come to know early on in our practice that our samsara ... the particular combination of neuroses that we suffer from ... is the result of our learned experience. Even fear, guilt, and shame are learned as children. We are products of our environment and upbringing, and our lives reflect the karma produced by the unskillful actions brought about by those neuroses.

Affirmations are designed to displace these negative learned feelings with positive ones that reflect our inner being, our true Buddha nature. Recognizing the power of our ego and the entrenched nature of these negative feelings, I began many years ago reciting affirmations together with other mantras each morning while doing my walking meditation prior to sitting.

Here are some examples of affirmations that either I have used or have given to others to use:

I, Ron, love, respect, and accept myself unconditionally.
YES, I love myself no matter what I do or have done, what I say or have said, what I possess, who I am with, whether I am alone, whether I am successful, whether I work — no matter what, I love and respect myself unconditionally and have compassion for myself. I believe in my true Buddha nature.

I, Ron, am a good person.

I, Ron, am loved, valued, and needed by others. My existence makes a difference in this world.

My feelings of inadequacy or failure reflect cultural or family judgments. They have no intrinsic existence; they are mere labels that are a product of my mind.

My inner being is always at peace and happy even when something happens to disturb me, just like the sun is always shining and the sky is always blue even when it is cloudy.

I continue to recite affirmations and mantras to this day because ones practice needs to be disciplined. One must be ever vigilant and aware of negative feelings that may still occasionally arise even after years of practice, especially in a moment of weakness.

Another organic approach to cultivating unconditional love and compassion for oneself is to follow the instructions of Sogyal Rinpoche and first "unseal the spring of loving kindness" towards yourself and then practice "tonglen" on yourself ... the Tibetan practice of taking on the suffering and pain of others and giving them your happiness, well-being, and peace of mind.[8] (This process is described in some detail on pp.96-97.) It is a very powerful tool I would recommend it be used in conjunction with affirmations.

Through our understanding of samsara, we come to an awareness of our, in a very basic sense, limited control over our lives when we may have thought we were quite in control of things. And we become aware that our self-image is actually a reflection of the image others have had of us, not a reflection of unfiltered reality ... for example, we may not make much money or have much, but we are not a "failure"; that is a label set by our culture, our peers, or our family.

Our awareness of these truths opens the intellectual door to feeling compassion and respect for ourselves. Yes, I am responsible for my life, but at a deeper level, until I broke out of the cycle of samsara by following the path, my ability to choose or reject and to see clearly was a limited one. Free will is in reality not free at all.

For the first time in our lives, when our ego throws negative words at us ... bad, stupid, unattractive, failure ... we understand that these are words that reflect the judgment of family, peers, or our culture – they do not reflect the real us – and that whatever we have done that we may feel remorse or regret for, those are things that often were not really within our control to do much otherwise. And so, we come to have the awareness that allows us to have compassion for ourselves, to love ourselves unconditionally.

But compassion does not stop with ourselves. We learn that all mankind in every corner of the earth, regardless how poor or how rich, regardless whether kind or cruel, regardless whether civilized or not, suffers from samsara.

---

[8] Sogyal Rinpoche, *The Tibetan Book of Living and Dying*, Harper Colllins, 1994

The details may be different in different people, but the experience of samsara is universal.

The awareness of the oneness of all humanity in its suffering opens the door to having compassion for all people. Even the Rwandan who wielded a machete or the Nazi SS guard who sent thousands to their death or the Charles Mansons of the world ... all of these individuals are deserving of compassion because they are victims of their own samsara. Regarding all one can truly say, "there but for the grace of God go I."[9]

Compassion and respect for all people ... and beyond that, for all sentient beings and the environment ... lies at the heart of Buddhism. It is the rock on which the Five Precepts rest. Every day when I prostrate myself, I invoke the Bodhisattva of Compassion with the Korean words, "Gwanseum bosal," and commit to cultivating a compassionate heart towards myself and all others.

---

[9] Jesus' statement from the cross is also very relevant, "Father forgive them for they know not what they do."

ACCEPTING LIFE

How do we find acceptance for our life, when we've spent our life not accepting it? It's like the old question of the chicken and the egg ... which comes first? Here the question is, is one only able to truly accept ones life as being the way it is right now after realizing the impermanence of all things and the illusory nature of all perceptions, or is acceptance an important initial step that makes it easier to meditate on the truths of impermanence and illusion?

This is not a trivial theoretical question. The answer has significant practical implications for the practitioner.

We are all victims of our cravings, our unskillful desires. While in the grip of those cravings, it is very hard for most people to "wrap their heads" around the concept of the illusory nature of all perceptions. We think we know the world and our condition in it. To not trust our mind, our senses, is a very unsettling proposition. And so, I made little if any progress towards this very important marker on the Buddhist path. My samsara continued unabated.

Even when in the grip of cravings, however, we are still usually capable in calmer moments of being aware of the wonderful things in our life ... be it our family, our job, our hobbies, our friends, the wonders of nature, the warmth of our bed, things large and small, whatever. I don't mean to be glib, but regardless how dissatisfied one is with ones life, there are always aspects that give us joy or that we feel good about when we stop and think about it. That certainly was true for me.

Is there a way of using that awareness to make progress on the path to accepting life? I believe the answer is, yes.

The first step I took was to work with this revealed fact. I focused on the good things in my life without saying, "Yes, but I don't have ... . " I tried to be aware of those things and be grateful for them ... but not attach to them ... throughout the day, especially when I got up in the morning and when I went to bed at night. Writing a short mantra for myself on this subject helped me focus.

When you have, if not turned your mind from your cravings, at least given the good things in your life equal time in your mind, then you are ready for the second step ... understanding the difference between skillful and unskillful desires.

One reason why we have a problem with acceptance is our fear of the unknown. "How will I pursue my life if I accept things as they are now?" Even if we understand that acceptance does not mean resignation, we think that acceptance entails letting go of our hopes and dreams. And the idea of that is unacceptable.

But that is not the case. Following the path does not mean letting go of all desires and hopes ... just unskillful ones. What turns an otherwise skillful desire into an unskillful one is often its origin in a lack of equanimity. Your desire may be in keeping with the five Precepts and thus skillful, but if it is based on your running from what is, if you are dissatisfied, then it becomes unskillful; it becomes a craving.

And what causes this lack of equanimity? Why do these hopes and dreams seem so elemental to our being that they create the destructive cravings that bring us only pain and frustration?

Hopes and dreams may be a function of human nature, but the lack of equanimity that transforms them into powerful cravings that cause suffering is caused by something else ... a lack of acceptance of ourselves, of who we are, and a lack of acceptance of our lives. If we do not have compassion for ourselves and love ourselves *unconditionally*, if we want to be something or someone other, we will suffer. If we are so blinded by cravings that we cannot see that we have what we need, what is most important to us,[10] right now, we will suffer. If we do not accept our lives, we will suffer.

So, if following the guidance of the previous section we have accepted ourselves, if we love ourselves unconditionally and have compassion for ourselves, then we are almost there; our equanimity has begun to blossom. If we just accept our life as it is right now, our equanimity will be complete and our skillful desires will remain skillful; our cravings and frustration will cease.

Once I understood this and that acceptance therefore does not mean consigning myself to a life in the future that is devoid of hopes and desires, then I was able to take the third step, which is to *truly* accept ... happily ... my life as being the way it is right now. These concepts are synergistic. This is not a mental trick; it is an honest way of resolving a very real obstacle to making progress on the path.

The change this brought about in my life cannot be overstated. As an example, for most of my life, I did not love myself unconditionally or have compassion for myself. And so I was obsessed with finding companionship, both for security and to feel wanted or loved. The perfectly healthy and skillful desire for friends or loved ones was transformed into a deep craving and frustration. My insecurity and anxiety were so extreme that even when I was in a relationship, I would be so afraid of losing it that my craving and frustration would continue unabated.

---

[10] And by "what we need" and "important" I mean whatever we experience at the moment that brings us well-being and joy, while realizing that all things are impermanent and not attaching to them. In other words, it's not the specific things we have at the moment, but the awareness that at any moment of any day of any year, there are things we experience that will bring us well-bring and joy ... whether they be things outside or inside of ourselves. Even in our darkest moments when our world may look very bleak, we know that those strengthening experiences are open to us if we are open to them.

But once I began to love myself unconditionally and have compassion, and began to accept my life as it was, knowing that I could still have skillful hopes and dreams, my demons deflated and my desire for companionship returned to its skillful state. I know now that my fear of being alone was just a function of the negative view I had of myself based on learned experience. There is no fear of being alone when you love yourself unconditionally and are at one with all things.

But beware, the line separating skillful and unskillful desires is very thin. It is difficult to both accept oneself and ones life and desire what one does not have; that is why the two are usually thought to be mutually exclusive and all desire is classified as unskillful. Desires have a way of pulling one away from ones acceptance. In order to keep our desires skillful, we must thus be disciplined in the practice of gratitude and acceptance until they are so deeply engrained that they become a paradigm of our life.

One also needs to be aware that because our ego and its cravings are so strong and wily, it is quite possible that when one reads these sections and responds positively to accepting oneself and ones life as it is, that acceptance will be merely an illusion, a self-deception. In that case, nothing will have changed and your cravings will be as strong and destructive as before. That is why I italicized the word "truly" when I wrote, "to *truly* accept my life."

What one needs to do in order to not fall into this trap is to give your acceptance some space and time to take root. This is after all a major shift for us after spending most of our lives not accepting. And we need to recognize that our craving for things is basically an addiction … we feel we need them to be happy … and so we need to follow the practice of 12-step programs and commit to not entertaining any of our desires/cravings for a period of time … however long it takes until you can honestly say that you accept yourself and your life as it is right now.

Your ego will certainly scream at you, "But I want [whatever]!" When it does that, you need to respond that you have what you need right now and you have faith that if you live each day well ... living a life in keeping with the Precepts ... the future will take care of itself. End of story!

Once many years ago, I asked a monk why, if we are all born essentially perfect, suffering was such a common human experience. His answer was, "It's just the way it is. It's like the law of thermodynamics."

When I heard his words it was like a huge burden was lifted from my shoulders. While acceptance was still key to maintaining my peace and serenity, that acceptance was made easier by understanding that things are the way they are because it's just the way they are. It wasn't really for me to accept; it just was. Again, these two concepts are synergistic. Once I had accepted myself as I am, I was able to truly accept that "it's just the way it is."

Having begun to free ourselves from the twin obstructions of dissatisfaction with our lives and craving what we don't have, we find that we are now able to practice the third Paramita ... patience ... and experience the abiding calm that comes with it.

As regards accepting the state of the world as it is right now, having accepted myself as I am, my compassion for all beings together with the teaching of "it's just the way it is" has altered the nature of my interaction with the news of the day and the world at large. No longer do I become angry and agitated. Instead I have concern and compassion.

As you focus on the wonderful things in your life and begin developing unconditional love and compassion for yourself and others, accepting your life as it is now, freeing yourself from unskillful desires, and practicing patience, then you will begin to experience the serenity and peace that is necessary to meditate on the twin truths of impermanence and the illusory nature of all perceptions. However long it may take to realize the emptiness of all five skandhas,[11] when you reach that state you will be open to surrendering your ego to your true Buddha nature and, as the Heart Sutra teaches, you will be at one with all things, experiencing things directly without the intervention of thought, thus ending doubt and suffering.

---

[11] The "five skandhas" are generally defined as the five physical and mental elements that comprise the existence of a person: form, feelings, perceptions, mental formations and consciousness. They are also referred to as "aggregates." The skandhas are discussed more fully and the definition tweaked and differentiated in Chapter 4 of my book, *The Self in No Self: Buddhist Heresies and Other Lessons of a Buddhist Life*.

STAYING GROUNDED

When I achieved a platform of serenity, the challenge was then to maintain it. In addition to continuing doing the things that brought me serenity as part of a disciplined daily practice, there was one more necessary element ... staying grounded.

As I make my way through life, there were and will be many challenges to my Buddhist practice and my serenity. I have found that this is especially true of anything that I put energy and effort into.

Until we reach a state of enlightenment, even if we have surrendered our ego to our true Buddha nature[12] and are in general at peace and content, feel at one with all things, are free of labels and attachments, and truly accept our life as it is, when we put effort into an activity, our ego often arises, looking to be stroked. And if it is not stroked, we get frustrated. (Of course if we haven't surrendered our ego, etc., the likelihood of our ego arising is just that much greater.)

Even if your desires are Right desires in that they are of skillful origination and in keeping with the Precepts and your efforts are self-less, ego still seems to arise when we are investing ourselves in some activity. Since putting forth effort is an integral part of living and indeed of Right effort, is there an answer to this conundrum?

Your initial reaction may be ... ah, this is a sign that I've been deceiving myself; I'm not truly accepting of my life or I'm not being truly self-less or I'm attached to this effort. While that may of course be true, it is not necessarily so.

It is an inherent part of human nature that when we put forth effort, we do it for a reason, for an end ... for example, to help others, to further our career, to resolve a

---

[12] For more on surrendering your ego, see the chapter, "Surrendering the Ego and Finding Peace."

problem, or just to learn or create something ... otherwise we would not put forth the effort to begin with. (NOTE: If you are doing such an activity because you feel the need to fix an inadequacy you feel, to "improve" yourself, then the activity is not skillful because it stems from a lack of equanimity that needs to be addressed.) And so, even if we truly accept our life, our ego often attaches unseen to such effort.

We learn that in pursuing a plan we should be present in the moment, not to attach, and not think about the future, about the outcome, but what if the present moment is a setback to our skillful effort? If we are not attached to our effort, we will say that it's just the way it is; the world will continue to move forward. It will not frustrate us. But if we have not been mindful and our ego arises and attaches to the effort, we will be frustrated.

For those efforts where, once we have produced something, we are dependent on others for its acceptance/use, a different dynamic occurs. Rather than letting it go at that point, not thinking about the future, we usually find ourselves consumed by doubt and desire during the seemingly eternal process of waiting for feedback and check our email or phone messages constantly for some word. This is very demoralizing and robs us of our peace.

The solution to this inescapable conundrum is to stay grounded. Whether it's your job, your volunteer work, or a book you're trying to write or market, you must make sure that the task does not consume you and rob you of your peace.

How we stay grounded depends on how far along you are with your practice. If you are at the point where you have developed the practice of being mindful and of nonattachment, then the answer is simply to be mindful, to be aware when the ego arises, to not engage it, and to confirm your nonattachment to the activity.

But if you are not at that point in your practice, you can stay grounded by first being present, which will allow you to be aware of the things and people that bring you joy, know that you have what you need, what is important to you right now, and maintain your focus in life on those things, as well as being disciplined in your practice of acceptance, compassion, loving yourself unconditionally, and meditation.

The key is to see your frustration or anger as a red flag ... it is your canary in a mine ... that one of two things is happening: either you are engaged in an activity or pursuing a goal which is not healthy for you, not consistent with the Five Precepts, or the activity or goal is in the abstract a healthy, skillful one, but you are approaching it in an unhealthy way, for example it is a craving that stems from a lack of equanimity.

When you experience frustration or anger, the first thing you must do is stop. Without stopping you cannot apply your spirituality to the situation. Center yourself by watching your breathing, using a technique as suggested in previous section on aware breath.

To determine whether the activity is just an ego trip or otherwise unhealthy, first ask yourself whether the activity is consistent with the Five Precepts. If it is, then ask, "Could this effort realistically make a difference?" The more macro the effort, the more likely that the answer to this question may be a painful, no. If it is either inconsistent with the Five Precepts or just an extension of your ego, then you need to drop the project to regain your sense of peace and contentment.

But if your effort really could make a difference, whether in one person's life or many, but the problem is that you are approaching it from a lack of equanimity, then ... since the assumption here is that you have not yet reached the state of practice where you are able to practice nonattachment ... you need to find a way to approach the activity in a healthy, non-craving way.

For most types of efforts you will help yourself stay grounded by limiting your time exposure to the activity. Keep your commitment appropriate with your focus on the things that bring you joy, that give you strength, and thus limit any potential negative impact.

You can't do that with your job, of course. Especially in today's work environment when there is often pressure to work almost 24/7.

But even here, you must not only carve out time for your family and other things that bring you joy ... those things must psychologically be the center of your life, not your work. It is a sad statement of our culture that for many people work has become their life; they live to work, not work to live.

A helpful compliment to maintaining the right focus in your life is to remember the truth ... it's just the way it is ... and meditate on that truth. Whatever is bothering you about the effort you are making, it's just the way it is.

It's also helpful to remember that we have no control over the future and can have no idea what is going to transpire ... therefore why obsess about what will happen? It's a no-win situation that robs you of your peace in the present, which is where you really need it. Instead, have faith that if you live each day well, in keeping with the five Precepts, the future will take care of itself.

Another tool that helps keep things in perspective is to engage in activities that relax you, calm you (beyond the spiritual ones already noted in this chapter). As adults, most of us have a real deficit in this area. Even activities that we supposedly do to relax us, to get away from things ... like playing golf, playing an instrument, shopping, whatever ... do not relax us because our ego is involved in those activities. They may be a distraction, but they are not calming.

What you need to do is some activity that puts you in touch with your inner child, that innocent being who was and is still free from the burdens of life and most learned experience. Most adults in our culture are closed off to their inner child; somehow it's not felt appropriate for adults to engage in childlike behavior or activities. And yet those activities, and the simple laughter that often accompanies them, give one access to the well of innocent joy that only a child experiences. Whether you used to love coloring books, climbing trees, playing with your dog (this is not to be confused with what adults do with their dogs in a dog park), or whatever, allow yourself the simple joy of immersing yourself in such activities with some regularity.

There is a deeper answer, however, to the question of how to stay grounded. There is a line in the classic Chinese poem, *Affirming Faith in Mind,* that says, "When the mind rests undisturbed then nothing in the world offends. And when no thing can give offense, then all obstructions cease to be."[13]

We are frustrated in these situations because our ego takes offense when we are not stroked. And the ego takes offense because these situations disturb our mind and our ego arises.

Why do these situations disturb our mind? Because for most of us they touch the deepest insecurities from our childhood about who we are, how we are valued, and whether we are liked or loved. Whenever we put ourselves, our talent, our credibility on the line, this ego insecurity is awakened.

If you've surrendered your ego to your true Buddha nature and are otherwise at one with all things, free of labels and obstructions, and if you love yourself unconditionally and have compassion for yourself, you may ask, "How can this still happen?" The answer is that unless, and perhaps

---

[13] Roshi Phillip Kapleau, *Chants*, Rochester Zen Center, 1990

even if, one is enlightened, your ego may be surrendered and you may love yourself unconditionally, but the ego does not disappear; it does not vanish from our existence; it remains part of us. It may no longer factor into our view of the world and our everyday lives ... but when our innermost insecurities are touched it arises and regains a foothold in our mind.

And so the deeper, more fundamental, solution to such frustration is to meditate on the truth that fear, guilt, and shame are learned. We must free ourselves from the past. Whatever made us feel insecure as children, that emotional reaction was a learned experience and does not reflect who we really were; it was a cultural or family judgment. And those judgments do not speak the truth; they are biased. Our cultural obsession with "improving" ourselves is not founded on a desire to learn more or do other things, it is based on a perception that we are inadequate in some way, that we are failures, and that that needs to be fixed. But we are not inadequate; we are not failures. These perceptions of ours have no intrinsic value; they are all of dependent origination. And so, being free of these perceptions and feelings or at least aware of their nature, we meditate on being at one with ourselves, experiencing ourselves without the intervention of thought. And we meditate on loving ourselves unconditionally, finding peace and hope in the present.

As noted above, even if you are at the point in your practice where you've surrendered your ego to your true Buddha nature, this can still happen; the ego can still arise. "How can that be?" you may ask. The ego does not disappear; it does not vanish from our existence; it remains part of us. It may no longer factor into our view of the world and our everyday lives ... but when our innermost insecurities are touched it can arise and regain a foothold in our mind. That is why we must be mindful, be aware when the ego arises, and confirm our nonattachment.

Free At Last

When I was a young man
I was consumed by a silent anger
Against the world and our culture.
I felt unwanted and unloved,
At times even despised, by others.
I could not accept the world as being
Just the way it is
Because I felt unfairly rejected by the world.
Feeling rejected,
I perversely rejected myself,
Believing what I was taught by the world.
And rejecting myself
Enflamed my anger all the more.

But when I found the Buddha dharma
I learned that I and all others were born
Essentially perfect
With the true Buddha nature
That remains intact throughout our lives.
The things that I had learned about myself,
All the labels, were false.
When I understood that my perceptions of
Myself were a product of the world
And not a product of who I was,
I was freed of these perceptions,
I believed in my true Buddha nature.
And when I believed in my true Buddha nature
I was able to love myself unconditionally and
Have compassion for myself;
I was able to accept myself just as I was.
And when I accepted myself just as I was
I was able to accept the world as being
Just the way it is
And have compassion for all people.

And when I accepted the world as it is
And found compassion for all people
I was freed from anger.
I felt sorrow and concern,
But I was free at last.

Chapter 3
Why Do We Crave? - The Root of All Suffering

When the Buddha set rolling the wheel of the dharma, he taught that the origin of suffering is craving ... craving for sensual desires, craving for being, craving for non-being.[14] In other words, regardless of the nature of the object of craving, craving causes suffering.

The cessation of suffering therefore lay in the "fading and ceasing, the giving up, relinquishing, letting go and rejecting of that same craving." And the way leading to this end of craving was the Noble Eightfold Path ... right view, right intention, right speech, right action, right livelihood, right effort, right mindfulness, and right concentration.[15]

In the Buddha's time, the Pali canon [16] contains example after example of individuals ... both monks and lay people ... who more or less instantaneously penetrated the dharma; "the spotless, immaculate vision of the Dharma arose" within them after receiving the Buddha's teaching. And who thereafter asked for and received full admission from the Buddha and became fully enlightened arahants.[17]

Likewise, millennia later, the record of the life and teachings of Zen Master Bankei (1622-1693) is full of examples of individuals who instantaneously became one

---

[14] Bhikkhu Nanamoli, *The Life of the Buddha*, BPS Pariyatti Editions, 1992, p.43
[15] ibid
[16] The canon contains the entire teachings of the Buddha, as they were related three months after his death and attainment of final nirvana. The canon is written in the language, Pali, which he spoke.
[17] Bhikkhu Nanamoli, op. cit., examples occur throughout the book; "full admission" refers to ordination as a Buddhist monk or nun.

with their unborn Buddha mind upon hearing his teaching and his exhortation to simply live in their unborn Buddha mind.[18]

Obviously something has changed in the intervening centuries ... we, at least in the West, do not hear about and we certainly haven't personally experienced this type of instantaneous enlightenment. Some might say that what has changed is the absence of truly great, holy teachers that one has the opportunity to have direct contact with. While that is certainly true for most of us, I don't think that's the critical part of the answer.

Rather, I think that what has changed is that modern man has a mental block to the teachings that people in historical eras did not. Part of that block lies in modern man's relationship with religion. In former eras, people easily opened up their hearts and souls to the teachings of religion. Even men of wealth and power were open to receiving the truth.

While certainly many people still fall into that category, many people have been turned off by religion, by the failure of its leaders and its teachings to work towards making this world a better place with less suffering. Instead, more violence and harm has been done in the name of religion over the centuries and continues to this day than probably any other force, including nationalism. Religion has lent its support to untold human injustices over the centuries. Many more are indifferent to religion; for them it is a matter of form not substance.

But that is still not the central issue here. The main thing blocking modern man, blocking us, to the teachings of the Buddha is the increased strength of the ego brought about by the changes in our culture, which at the same time has increased the strength of our cravings.

---

[18] Norman Waddell, op. cit.

The ego of course has always been a problem ... witness the Buddha's struggles to find enlightenment and the ongoing temptations presented by Mara, his spiritual tempter. But in modern Western culture, man has evolved from a being subject to certain basic fears and desires that were part of the human condition into a being subject to an incredibly complex and strong panoply of fears and desires formed by the prevailing culture and our learned experience. We have morphed into something almost totally out of control ... which is to say with our ego in full control ... and without any awareness of that fact. For many, hell is found in living. "Progress" has not been kind to the human condition.

And so we find that even the gate to following the Noble Eightfold Path is closed to us because in order to practice the Noble Eightfold Path one must first be free of ego. One cannot practice Right View or Right anything ... becoming a stream-enterer ... if ones ego, ones learned experience, is still an active force in ones mind, because the ego will intervene by generating thoughts/obstructions which commandeer our mind and obscure our true Buddha nature, from which flows the various Right activities.

For modern man, at least modern Western man, the essential task thus becomes one of freeing oneself from ones ego. To approach that task, we must first have clarity about the cause of our craving and the role of our ego. I do not mean here an individualistic psychoanalytical view of our cravings and our ego, but rather a more macro generic view of these forces.

Since our minds are not open to the kind of spiritual conversion seen in the past, we must approach the process first from an intellectual perspective. Once we have convinced our mind, and thus ourselves, of the truth of the teachings on an intellectual level, our mind and heart will be open to taking the truths the further step and embracing them fully, internalizing them.

So let us begin. We know that craving is the cause of our suffering, but why do we crave? The quick answer is that we crave because we are attached to things. Alright. But that begs the question then of why are we attached to things.

We attach to things because we are not at peace, we have little or no equanimity. Regardless of our position, high or low, we are so unsettled in the deepest recesses of our mind and gut that we grasp at the things that we do ... whether it's work, hobbies, love, whatever ... to rescue us from this state of turmoil. Achievement of these goals becomes the central essence of life for us. It is what gives our life meaning and purpose. We always want what we don't have, and when we get it, it's never enough.

This is the essence of craving. The result is inevitable disappointment, frustration, and suffering. We are never able to sincerely say to ourselves, "job well done," and take satisfaction in that. If what we want doesn't come to pass, we're not able to say, "Well, that's just the way it is. I and the world will go on just fine without that."

Even being aware of this and its impact on our samsara does not result in any deliverance for us. We must go deeper. Why do we have this lack of equanimity, this inner turmoil? If we were all born essentially perfect with the true Buddha nature inside us, why do we suffer so?

In part, as discussed in the previous chapter, we lack equanimity because we do not accept ourselves and our lives as they are right now at this moment. But that once again begs the question of why.

We cannot accept ourselves and our lives because of the fears and insecurities that developed within us, usually during childhood. These fears and insecurities in turn were learned experiences, were the result of experiences we had interacting either with our family, our peers, or the larger society and culture. We ended up defining ourselves and the world around us through a bundle of learned labels, which blocked our mind and heart from the knowledge of who we and who the world around us really were.

Think about how you define yourself in terms of your level of occupational or financial achievement, your looks, your intellectual ability. You will see that you use labels to define yourself ranging from success to failure, from handsome to ugly, from smart to dumb. The same applies to all aspects of yourself. And if you are honest, you will see that even if you label yourself in a positive way on most attributes, there is one or more on which you label yourself negatively, and it is the negative labels that end up overpowering the others and forming your definition of yourself. How you view and thus interact with the world around you is also defined by such labels.

How did you come to choose these labels to define everything? It may seem to you that it was a conscious decision you made, but that is not the case. The choice was made for you by your family or your peers or the larger society. All these groups set the parameters of what is good or bad, what is desirable or not desirable.

Being a part of your family, peer-group, and the larger society, you adopted those parameters automatically already as a child ... at times these groups do not agree on the parameters, in which case one adopts the parameters set by the group one feels closest to, which can change over the years ... or they were directly applied to you and you accepted the application. As the song from *South Pacific* so wisely says, "You've got to be taught before it's too late, before you are six or seven or eight, to hate all the people your relatives hate, you've got to be carefully taught."[19]

The first step in the process of freeing ourselves from our suffering is to acknowledge this basic fact of our lives. Once we acknowledge that our perceptions are all a function of our family, peer-group, or larger society and that

---

[19] Richard Rodgers and Oscar Hammerstein II, *South Pacific*, "You've Got To Be Carefully Taught," Hal Leonard Corporation, 1981

it is these perceptions that make it impossible for us to truly accept ourselves and our lives as they are, to love ourselves unconditionally and have compassion for ourselves, which in turn makes it impossible to approach our lives with equanimity, which in turn causes us to attach to what we do and thus crave those things, which is the cause of our suffering … once we acknowledge all of this, then we have positioned ourselves to address the next steps. Then we can start the process of freeing ourselves from the chains of our learned experience, from our ego, and thus end our suffering.

But how to free ourselves from our ego? Many Buddhist teachers do not address this matter directly. Those that face the power of our ego head on, such as Sogyal Rinpoche, teach that as our discriminating awareness strengthens through meditation, we begin to distinguish clearly between the guidance of our true Buddha nature and our ego.[20] Eventually, the destructiveness of our ego will be clear and that will release us. Similarly, Krishnamurti calls for a "revolution of the psyche" and posits that understanding our conditioning/ego immediately without thought allows us to be free of that conditioning.[21]

Yet many have reached such realization and still remain bound by their egos; it is that powerful and wily. Recognizing the difficulty and the centrality of this action to leading a Right life and ending our suffering, the teaching that I received from the Vietnamese Zen monk, the Ven. Huyen Te (and later, the Ven. Thai Tue), focused on a more defined path to free ourselves from our ego. I think of this teaching as the Missing Noble Truth and it is the core of what I call the Fourfold Path to Freedom:

---

[20] Sogyal Rinpoche, op. cit..
[21] J. Krishnamurti, *Freedom From the Known*, HarperSanFrancisco, 1968

Understanding that all things are impermanent and changeable.
Understanding the illusory/empty nature of all perceptions.
Practicing the Six Paramitas.
Surrendering our ego to our true Buddha nature.

Most of the teaching contained in this Fourfold Path is found in different Buddhist teachings: the Two Truths – relative and worldly; the Three Dharma Seals – impermanence, non-self, and nirvana; and the Three Doors of Liberation – emptiness, absence of labels, and just being.

Willfully choosing to surrender ones ego, however, as opposed to altering specific activities or thoughts, or being freed of the ego by understanding it's destructiveness, is not a traditional Buddhist concept.[22] Interestingly, it is a core concept in 12—step recovery programs, which borrow many elements from Buddhist teaching.

By focusing on just a few key elements of traditional teaching and culminating with the choice to surrender ones ego, my teachers created a practical and powerful path to enable us to be free of our ego and thus practice the Noble Eightfold Path, ultimately freeing us from our suffering.

We start with understanding that our perception of all things are empty of intrinsic existence.

---

[22] Although the Buddha's statement of the Third Noble Truth, noted earlier, appears consistent with the concept of willful surrender, other language in the dharma is more consistent with Sogyal Rinpoche's approach noted above. I think the concept is, however, closely related to the teachings of Zen Master Bankei on the Unborn. When Bankei would tell people that they were creatures of their partiality [ego] and that they should simply live in their unborn Buddha-mind, while the language was different, it was in essence the same as Huyen Te telling us to surrender our egos to our true Buddha nature. Norman Waddell, op. cit.

Chapter 4
Discovering the Emptiness of Thought

It is one thing to acknowledge that all of our perceptions are based on learned experience. It is quite another to acknowledge and understand that those perceptions are illusory, that they and our learned experience are empty of intrinsic existence and thus do not reflect reality ... that we have no way of experiencing reality through the faculty of our mind.

The easiest way to see the truth in this Buddhist maxim is a practical one ... look at the experiences of your everyday life. For example, think of almost any element of weather ... heat, cold, rain, snow. These are very objective, measurable facts. Yet one person will thrive in a particular weather condition while another can't stand it. Our reactions to the weather are entirely subjective and change from person to person.

What causes these differing reactions? It's our learned experience. Whether it's the weather we grew up with, whether it's how our parents or peers reacted to the weather ... a variety of learned inputs form our individual response to the weather.

And this subjective view in turn causes many of us suffering. How often have we been in a weather situation that we didn't like ... whether high heat and humidity or unrelenting rain or snow ... which had the psychological impact of making us miserable and depressed?

What has happened is that our learned experience has caused us to put mental labels on everything that we experience ... labels that something is good or bad ... which interfere with our perception of the true quality of things. When a sensory image goes from the eyes, nose, or ears to the brain, it is these labels that impact how the images are received. Our conscious mind does not receive them neutrally.

The point here is that heat, rain, cold, snow, etc. are neither good nor bad ... they just are. And they are all an essential part of our environment, of our ecological system. Our perception of the "lousy" weather may seem very real to us, but it's all a function of our mind and thus illusory, not a reflection of reality. Take away the labels and we can perceive the value and wonder of all types of weather, with the possible understandable exception of natural disasters.[23]

So it is with all things in life. We cannot know the true nature of things because the labels in our mind interfere with how we perceive all things.

For example, feelings of being inadequate or a failure, as well as all our various neuroses, are a function of how we view ourselves based on our learned experience ... whether that comes from family, friends, peers, or the larger culture. Hard as it may be to accept, such feelings are thus not a reflection of the reality of who we are; they are illusory perceptions.

To be clear, this assertion does not dispute the fact, for example, that we are unemployed, or making a certain amount of money, or tend to be introverted ... it disputes the label our mind places on those conditions. And the fact that our culture supports that label makes it no less illusory; it makes it *seem* very real and makes it harder to free ourselves from that perception, but it is still just a creation of our mind based on our learned experience.

Let us take this a step further to the realm of ideas. I used to be a type "A" personality and believed that I was

---

[23] But even in the case of a disaster, having no labels and understanding that it's just the way it is changes how we react to it. And if it's partly caused by human activity, we can work to change that human activity, but always from a position of equanimity and compassion.

always right ... that my opinions were the right ones and anyone who disagreed with me was wrong.

Once I understood that all our perceptions are illusory, that meant that my view of all things in life was illusory ... caused by the various learned experiences I had had. Other people, however ... for example, someone on the other side of a discussion ... might come to a different view of things, a different opinion based on their learned experiences.

And so, while I still had opinions/thoughts (until one is further on the path and can observe and perceive without the intervention of thought, ones illusory perceptions are all one has to go by), I did not attach to them ... I did not label mine as right and others wrong. Rather I respected that most people come to their opinions honestly and that all opinions deserve respect. [24] From that point onward, discussions I had with people who had opposing views to my own had a very different dynamic and were much more productive.

But perhaps the most common and destructive illusion we all have in our culture is the thought or dream that we would be happier if only we had what we do not have. Yet we know from our own experience and from psychological studies that attaining what we thought would make us happy doesn't do the trick ... at least not for more than a short period of time. And so unskillful desire is just another form of attachment to an illusion that causes us suffering by making us feel dissatisfied with our present, making us obsess about the future, and then causing us dissatisfaction all over again.

---

[24] I should note that in Buddhism there are things that are not morally consistent with the path – generally stated, harming others ... killing, stealing, sexual misconduct, and lying, for example. But one still has compassion towards people who conduct themselves in such a manner for they are but a product of their learned experience. For more, see the earlier section, "Accepting Ourselves."

Looked at another way, the destructive force of this illusion is that it diverts us from being aware of all the wonderful things in our life right now at this moment and being grateful. And without that awareness, it is much more difficult if not impossible to accept ones life as being the way it is right now, without which otherwise skillful desires and hopes turn into unskillful desires and cravings.[25]

Another area in which we suffer from the impact of illusory perceptions is our view of the permanence of things. Whether it's something good that we don't want to end or it's something bad that we can't imagine ever ending, we have in the one instance a craving for permanence and in the other an illusion of permanence.

Yet if there is one thing that is certain in life, it is that all things are impermanent and changeable. The statement that all things that rise, fall, is a central tenet of the Buddha dharma.

Here again, we have but to look at nature to see the truth of this fact. Nature is an endless cycle. Whether we look at the cycle of plants or the weather, the lesson is one of constant change and renewal. Plants bloom, go dormant or die, and throw off seed to perpetuate their kind. The endless series of gray cold days in winter give way to the sunny warmer days of spring and summer, which before long will grow shorter and colder as winter nears again. The waves breaking on the beach and disappearing become waves again through the cycle of the water's flow, the wind, and the tides.

No matter where we look, there is really no beginning or end, just an endless unbroken cycle. So it is also with human life ... all things are impermanent and changeable ... and while there is a physical beginning and end, the expression "dust to dust, ashes to ashes" expresses that here

---

[25] For a discussion of this see the section "The Desire That is Right Desire" in my previously published book, *The Self in No Self: Buddhist Herisies and Other Lessons of a Buddhist Life.*

too the change is part of a larger endless cycle. Understanding that reality and accepting it would remove much of our suffering.

But we humans do not immerse ourselves in that wisdom. Instead, we attach to what is present in our lives at the moment or was in the past, whether it be something that we view as good or bad. And we obsess about either's permanence in the future. This causes us needless suffering.

In the first instance, we suffer when we have something we view as good ... whether it be someone we love, or a good job, or financial success ... because we attach to its permanence and have an obsessive fear of losing what we have in the future. That creates anxiety and stress, which makes enjoying what we have in the moment almost impossible. In the second instance, we suffer because we view something in our lives as bad and cannot imagine it ever changing because we again attach to it.

But whether it's despair or elation, both are impermanent and changeable. Indeed, the very experience of "despair" or "elation" is yet another example of illusory perceptions caused by the mental labels that we attach to the things that we experience.

In both situations, if we were mindful of the impermanence of all things, if that was our expectation, then we would not obsess about loosing something we valued or continue to be burdened with something from the past that causes pain. We would just focus on the present, because that is all there is, and make the most of the present moment.

"Nonsense," you say, "if I believed that and couldn't count on my marriage or any of the things I value lasting into the future, I would be a neurotic mess." But that's because you are trapped in the habit of seeking permanence. If you were freed of that habit energy, you would be at peace.

There is one fact of impermanent existence, however, that more than any other impacts how we live our lives ... death. Each of us knows that at some point we will die ... our lives will end. But most of us do not really accept that fact ... we are typically in denial of our own mortality ... and, in our culture at least, most have a fear of death. Again, examples of illusory perceptions.

After the death of my partner from AIDS, I certainly was no longer in denial of my own mortality; indeed, I was very aware of it. But I still had a fear, actually a greater fear, of death. And that fear made it impossible to be happy in the present because it fed my attachment to things present and future.

When instead I understood and accepted that I may die at any moment ... perhaps tonight ... and was ready for that eventuality free of fear because I understood the illusory nature of my perceptions of death[26], only then was I able to truly be present and take joy in each passing moment. Only then can we all be free of our attachment and obsession with the future.

With a general understanding that all perceptions are illusory and all things are impermanent and changeable, one slowly begins to release attachments and be more mindful, more aware during the day ... to experience things, to observe, directly without the intervention of thought, without labels. When thoughts do rise, we are more aware of this and of their illusory nature, and so we watch them rise and fall; we do not engage them, we do not attach to them. And the more one experiences things with equal mind (for most of us this is not an all at once thing, it is

---

[26] The physical pain I saw when my partner died was real, but my perception of death as a horrible wrenching event ... think of the common portrayal of death with his scythe ... was based on my not being able to separate the physical pain from my thought of the pain and from my own suffering at his loss. What the experience of death is like is something that we, the living, cannot know. It is what it is.

incremental), the more our suffering and doubt cease. For during those moments, we see ourselves and the world around us unencumbered by ego and are at one with all things.

But if our thoughts are empty of intrinsic existence, what then about the objects and aspects of life that are the subject of our thoughts? Just as our thoughts are of dependent origin and thus are empty of intrinsic meaning, so to are all objects and aspects of life of dependent origination and thus empty of intrinsic existence. Whether it's z vein of coal, a blade of grass, or the ebb and flow of politics or relationships ... all these things are of dependent origination. Coal exists because of a process that started millions of years ago; grass exists because of seed that was deposited; life happens one way or another because of factors that impact it. All are examples of cause and effect, of dependent origination; if the causal factors weren't present, the things would not exist, or not in their present form. And thus all are empty of intrinsic existence.

The physical world and the world as experienced through our thoughts are therefore two parallel and interacting tracks of cause and effect, of dependent origination. When we understand this "emptiness" deeply, our whole frame of reference for experiencing ourselves and the world around us changes.

Let me illustrate with a seemingly nonsensical statement: One can only find security when one realizes that there is no such thing as security. I have spoken about my obsession with the future, permanence, and happiness and the suffering that comes from the inevitable frustration caused by that obsessive search. Living in the wisdom of Buddhism, I came to understand that there is no security (as we think of it) because all things are impermanent and our perceptions illusory. Once I realized that, I was freed from the search for security. And once I was freed from the search for security, I was truly secure ... because I found peace and happiness in the present.

If all our thoughts are empty of intrinsic existence and if all physical objects and aspects of life are empty of intrinsic existence, then what, you may well ask, does reality consist of? This conundrum is made even more perplexing by the common Buddhist teaching that says that all things are empty, or that they are void.

To a person schooled in the English language, those words mean that there is nothing there. This formulation caused a significant barrier to my understanding and progress because I thought, "How can the monk say that the cup he's holding up doesn't exist? It makes no sense."

At first blush, this formulation may seem consistent with the related teaching that all perceptions are illusory. However, that is not the case. The point is that *perceptions* are illusory ... because our senses are first filtered through our thoughts and thus are a function of our learned experience, of dependent origination ... not that the things themselves, the objects of our perception, are non-existent.

Taking the cup example, when we see the object, our perception is illusory because when we look at it we apply labels seemingly without thought ... it's large or small, attractive or ugly. But the cup the monk is holding does physically exist.[27]

If a person cuts himself or has a late stage cancer, that person will experience pain, and that pain is real; it exists. However, when the person thinks about the pain, when thought creates fear, depression, or other feelings, those thoughts are likewise illusory, those perceptions of the real pain are products of the mind; and that is suffering.

---

[27] There is of course another way in which our sense of the physical form is illusory because our senses themselves are limited. Our unaided eyes can only see the appearance of the outer form of the physical object; we are not able to see the actual physical structure of the cup, which is in reality very different from the smooth surface our eyes see.

Another way of explaining this is to say that one cannot stop pain once the causal factor has occurred (short of taking drugs), but one can be free of feelings of fear or depression that our mind creates from that pain.

The words "empty" and "void" therefore turn out to be bad choices in translating this central Buddhist concept. Recognizing this, much Buddhist teaching uses the phrase "empty of intrinsic existence," as I have in this book. Whether one is speaking of the base skandhas/aggregates, or the aggregates as affected by clinging, they are empty of intrinsic existence; they are of dependent origination.[28]

If one cannot experience reality through the faculty of our mind, how then does one experience reality? The key is to experience things without the intervention of thought, which is to say purely through the senses, and that in turn is only possible when one understands the emptiness of all five skandas, is free of ego, and thus is at one with all things. At that stage of practice ... the object of this book ... we are able to experience the sense world whole and complete, just as it is.[29]

In the meantime, one can experience glimpses of that reality when one is mindful and observes free of thought; remember this is an incremental process. After reading this chapter and meditating on its teaching you will hopefully have a good practical grasp of the illusory nature of all

---

[28] Throughout the discourses, the Buddha refers to both "aggregates" and "clinging aggregates." The difference is that the five aggregates just are ... if one doesn't attach to them they pose no problem. Even the Buddha states that he has feelings, perceptions and thoughts, but he doesn't attach to them and thus they do not impact him. Bhikkhu Nanamoli, *The Life of the Buddha*, BPS Pariyatti Editions, 1992, p.5

[29] As the Buddha instructs in the Bahiya Sutta, "when there is only the seen in reference to the seen, the heard in reference to the heard, the cognized in reference to the cognized, there is no you in terms of that." Bhikkhu Thanissaro, "Bahiya Sutta: About Bahiya" (Ud 1.10), *Access to Insight*, 8 July 2010, http://www.accesstoinsight.org/tipitaka/kn/ud/ud.1.10.than.html

perceptions and the impermanence of all things. Now it is important to put that teaching into practice.

My Vietnamese teachers, Huyen Te and Thai Tue, stressed that key to following the Fourfold Path to Freedom is the process of observing. As we went through our days, we were taught to observe both what we saw or heard, as well as what we were doing, without the intervention of thought. For example, if I was driving through the countryside, instead of looking at the scenery and thinking how pretty it was, or what an interesting tree that was, running a mental commentary on it, I would just observe with no thought; if a thought arose, I would watch it arise and fall, I would not attach to it and engage it. Likewise, if I was in a conversation with someone, I would observe myself like a neutral third party. In these moments, it felt like I was disembodied ... like a separate part of me was observing free of my body.

In the early stages of this process, this ability to observe, to be mindful, happened only fleetingly and was often willed. But as time went on and my practice deepened further, the ability to observe expanded and became second nature, almost my default mode, till at some point I saw *most*[30] things as they truly are, free of my illusory perceptions because I understood, not just intellectually but at my core, that these things are impermanent and changeable and that my perceptions of them are illusory.

For now, whenever you are not able to observe without the intervention of thought, be mindful that our perceptions are illusory and that reality as we perceive it may be quite different from reality as it truly is. Do not attach to your perceptions and put the stamp of reality upon them.

---

[30] I say "most" things because for many years I continued to be unable to observe those things that engaged the core of my ego free of thought, free of my ego.

Chapter 5
Practicing the Six Paramitas

The Fourfold Path to Freedom requires not just great discipline, but the development of powerful compassion towards oneself and all others. Without that compassion, one cannot truly surrender your ego to your true Buddha nature and be at one with it, selfless.

But since we human beings are largely controlled by our ego, until such time as we free ourselves from it we are in a "catch-22" because our ego leaves little room for compassion for ourselves or others, and yet that is what we must develop in order to free ourselves from our ego. To move forward on the path, we therefore need all the help we can get in stepping out of our egocentric mentality.

The Five Precepts is certainly an exercise in compassion and selflessness and an essential place to start. But to deepen our practice, it is very helpful to practice the Six Paramitas.

The Six Paramitas are ... generosity, virtuous conduct, understanding, enthusiastic effort and diligence, meditation/concentration, and wisdom. To practice these teachings, often referred to as the Six Perfections,[31] is to water the seeds of our true Buddha nature, which has been obscured by our ego and learned experience. Thus although these qualities are inherent parts of all of us, we need to cultivate them and bring them to the surface of our consciousness. As we develop these qualities ... and in that

---

[31] This is a less-than-helpful translation from Sanskrit into English. To the English- speaker, the noun "perfection" means flawlessness or excellence. Instead the meaning of "paramita" here is "quality/virtue that aids in crossing from samsara to nirvana," and so is to be perfected or cultivated. The noun and verb are not interchangeable.

sense "perfect" them ... we decrease our suffering and increase our awareness, freedom from our ego, and happiness.

In approaching this practice, it is critical, as with the Five Precepts, that they be approached with equanimity and loving kindness. If one is generous, or ethical, or any of the six qualities not just for the sake of practicing generosity, etc., but instead to feel good about being generous or be valued for being generous or create an image of being generous, then you are not practicing the paramita because your activity is unskillful, stemming from an ego-desire. Others may still benefit from your activity, but your lack of equanimity negates the merit that would otherwise have been received. You will thus not experience any greater freedom or happiness.

The fact that our ego has the ability to co-opt otherwise skillful activity is frustrating, but very common. As stated previously in the section on "Staying Grounded" and in the chapter, "How To Plan Yet Remain Present," in my book, *Making Your Way In Life as a Buddhist,* one must be always on the watch for the ego's attempt to corrupt a selfless activity. No matter how far along you are in your practice, constant discipline and mindfulness is the order of the day.

GENEROSITY

Generosity sounds like a pretty straightforward matter. I mean, we all know what it means, right? And we all practice it, at least to some extent. But do we really understand what generosity means in the Buddhist context and do we practice it?

There are two aspects of generosity in Buddhism that are equally important ... the one is the act and the other is the origination of the act. I have already spoken in the introduction to this section about the importance of an act of generosity originating from a state of equanimity and a spirit of unconditional loving kindness and compassion for all.

It's probably safe to say that most of the generosity that is practiced in this world originates from a different place, one driven by ego or pity. The most common acts of generosity are the giving of money, whether to charity or directly to someone in need, and the giving of time by volunteering with an organization that helps people in need.

But the giving of money and the giving of time are the easiest forms of generosity because they require the least of us spiritually. This is not to downplay their value ... you can definitely change peoples lives for the better through both these acts of generosity ... but these acts can be practiced without them originating in loving kindness and compassion for all people. Indeed, these acts of generosity, because they can be practiced from a variety of motives, can easily give one the feeling of being generous, when in a Buddhist sense one isn't.

The other type of generosity involves literally giving of oneself, and that is not possible without it originating in a skillful way ... well perhaps it is, but it is less likely. This type of giving stems from your very presence. When you give someone understanding, a sense of peace, a feeling of stability, or the freedom from fear through your actions and words, by listening deeply and speaking with loving kindness, or bring joy into their lives, then you have truly given of yourself. And while the practice of giving money or time is by necessity limited in scope for most of us, giving of ourselves can be done numerous times on a daily basis towards family, friends, and strangers.

Now as I intimated, it is certainly possible for the ego to co-opt even these types of actions. Even if they originated in a self-less, loving way, the ego can transform the motivation into one more to its benefit and cause attachment to arise. So be aware.

Think about the acts of generosity that you have performed in the recent past. Meditate on what the origination of those acts were. If they stemmed from something other than unconditional loving kindness and compassion, it they did not stem from a state of equanimity, then at least that awareness will be helpful to you as you move forward on the path. Self-knowledge leads to growth; self-deception results in stagnation.

VIRTUOUS CONDUCT

Virtuous or ethical conduct is something for which we don't have many good role models in our secular culture. For all the countless examples in business, politics, the professions, and other walks of life that we hear of on a daily basis in which people have acted in an unethical manner, there are multitudes of similar actions that are unknown and unreported. What that says of our culture is sad ... that for many people the ends do justify the means.

But in this as in so many other ways, those who choose to follow the Buddhist path listen to a different drummer. For us, virtuous or ethical conduct is one of the core principles in living life as a Buddhist. The second paramita can be defined in various ways. In addition to virtuous or ethical conduct, it entails morality, personal integrity, and doing no harm to other sentient beings.

It is this last aspect that is the essence of the second paramita ... doing no harm to others or indeed to oneself. And we can best practice and "perfect" virtuous conduct by following the Five Precepts ... not killing, helping others, refraining from sexual misconduct, speaking and listening with loving kindness, and not consuming things which are harmful.

The first Precept states: "Aware of the suffering caused by the destruction of life, I am committed to cultivating compassion and learning ways to protect the lives of people, animals, plants, and minerals."[32] Note that this, and all of the Precepts as presented by Thich Nhat Hanh, begins with a statement of awareness. We are not told to follow these moral guidelines because they are a commandment; rather, we are asked to be aware of the suffering of others, and out of that awareness act so as to help end or at least lessen such suffering.

---

[32] The versions of the Precepts quoted here are all taken from, or adapted from those found in Thich Nhat Hanh's *The Heart of the Buddha's Teaching*, Parallax Press, 1998.

The area where this precept has the most practical application for most of us is in the question whether or not to eat meat and fish, whether to support the killing of animals for the benefit of man's appetite. Most of us grew up as meat-eaters. That is the prevailing culture ... our parents, our friends, virtually everyone around us were meat-eaters. The taste of a good steak or roast or stew, the juiciness of a good hamburger, and for me, all the wonderful German cold-cuts ... the idea of doing without these was one of the hardest things to accept when I thought about living life as a Buddhist.

Both the temples I attended ... a Korean Zen and a Vietnamese Zen were strictly vegetarian. So I thought that being a Buddhist meant being vegetarian ... until I had my first meal with some Tibetan monks and saw them eat meat!

This is truly the "to be or not to be" question in Buddhism. And there is no clear answer, as the various branches of Buddhism ... Theravada, Mahayana, and Vajrayana ... have different teachings on the subject. The subject is so esoteric and confused that I will not even attempt to make sense of the conflicting viewpoints.

Since the teachings of the Buddha on this subject are in dispute, with one school saying that the eating of meat is not consistent with the practice, at least certainly for monks, while another says that it is, at least for lay people and under many conditions even for monks, I would say that one has choices here.

If your practice follows a particular lineage that has a definite teaching on this subject, then it would seem that it would be best to follow those teachings. However, if you, like me, do not follow any particular lineage, then I suggest that making a decision is a question of ethics.

Killing an animal or any sentient being is in most circumstances the polar opposite of protecting life, of acting with loving kindness towards a person or being. Clearly one cannot say, "But I really enjoy eating meat and fish." Ones pleasure does not support taking the life of another sentient being. That is not a mitigating context.

A critical question for me was, is eating meat and fish necessary or helpful to maintaining health? As a person living with a compromised immune system, this question was very important to me.

The unequivocal answer after reviewing various sources is, no. Eating a vegetarian diet that includes eggs and dairy products not only provides all the nutrients needed for good health (with perhaps an occasional fish dish thrown in) but studies uniformly show that vegetarians are more healthy and live longer than non-vegetarians. There is no health-related reason to eat meat and fish. Indeed, quite the opposite is true.

Is there some other way to justify eating meat and fish without breaking the first Precept? Even if you eat solely free-range meat and wild-caught fish, and even if the animals are killed in a humane way, from an ethical standpoint it makes no difference. Killing is still violence; a taking of life. These animals are still being killed to feed you.

Which brings up one last possible way to justify eating meat and fish. Theravada Buddhism teaches that the Buddha allowed monks to eat meat that was received as part of their alms if they did not know or suspect that the meat was killed specifically for them. One could say that when one buys meat and fish in the supermarket, it certainly is not killed specifically for you. Therefore, it could be eaten.

As a meat and fish eater at the time I began writing this book, and having believed prior to doing the research for this section that there were health justifications for doing so, and I must say loving to cook and eat meat and fish, I was torn as to the path to take in the future. But from an ethical standpoint, I could not see my way clear to justifying my continuing to eat meat and fish.

The "out" that I just noted above about it not being killed specifically for me just doesn't seem valid. Yes, we live in a meat-eating society and whether I eat meat or not is not going to save any animals. But one could say the same thing for the entirety of Buddhist practice ... it is out of step with the rest of our culture and yet we follow the precepts because it is the right thing to do. And although my actions may not change the world, it will change me, remove a catalyst of my samsara, and perhaps influence those with whom I am in direct contact.

Which brings up the point of what to do when invited to someone's house? I believe in being a gracious guest; in this context, I eat what is prepared by my host, regardless whether I like it or it conforms to my belief-system. Also, when I'm traveling and don't have options for good substitute protein sources, I do eat meat and fish, for health reasons.

And so, with those exceptions and an occasional fish dish as noted above, from the day I am writing this forward, I commit to being a lacto-ovo vegetarian. My life in all respects will be consistent with the first Precept.

The other area in which the first Precept has very practical consequences is our action in time of war. The simplest form of the first Precept is, "do not kill," and indeed Thich Nhat Hanh's version continues with a vow not just not to kill but to not in any way support killing by others. I did not include this language in my version noted above because that sounds like pacifism, and while the Buddha taught non-violence, it was not absolute and he did not teach pacifism.

I once asked a monk if one could kill a mosquito and not break the first Precept. His response was that the Precepts are not mindless of context. If one is acting in self-defense ... such as killing a mosquito ... then one hasn't broken the first Precept. The same concept would apply in war, if your country is attacked; if the war is undertaken to protect lives rather than out of hatred for others, then war and participating in war is not inconsistent with being a lay Buddhist.[33]

The Buddha dharma is full of stories of the Buddha interacting with warrior-kings. Never once in his teachings did the Buddha admonish these individuals or instruct them to cease conducting wars or committing violence to protect the lives and wellbeing of their people. If one, on the other hand, had been ordained into the sangha of bhikkhus, then one would be expected to participate in no act of violence. Different people have different roles and responsibilities in life; the Buddha recognized this.

The second Precept state, "Aware of the suffering caused by exploitation, social injustice, stealing, and oppression, I am committed to cultivating compassion and loving kindness towards myself and all others and learning ways to work for wellbeing of people, animals, plants, and minerals. I will practice generosity by sharing time, energy, and material resources with those who are in real need." After our discussion of the first Paramita, I don't think more needs to be said.

The third Precept states, "Aware of the suffering caused by sexual misconduct, I am committed to cultivating responsibility and learning ways to protect the safety and integrity of individuals, couples, families, and society. I am determined not to engage in sexual relations without love and a long-term commitment. To preserve the happiness of myself and others, I am determined to respect my commitments and the commitments of others." In today's

---

[33] As one teacher put it: "Can you do this task as an upholder of safety and justice, focused on love of those you protect rather than on hate for those you must kill? If you are acting with vengeance or delight in destruction, then you are not at all a student of Dhamma. But if your hard job can be done with a base of pure mind, while you are clearly not living the life of an enlightened person, you are still able to begin walking the path towards harmony and compassion." Paul Fleishman, "The Buddha Taught Nonviolence, Not Pacifism," http://www.dharma.org/ij/archives/2002a/nonviolence.htm

culture, this Precept is for most people probably the most challenging of all because it is without question contrary to our culture's current norms.

Obviously, "friends with benefits," casual sex, even sex in a short-term dating context is considered sexual misconduct under this standard. I should note that other interpretations of the third Precept are less restrictive than Thich Nhat Hanh's. I asked a Theravadan monk what constitutes sexual misconduct and he said that as long as it was between consenting adults, sex was ok and there was no misconduct.

In thinking about this Precept, it is most important to remember that the primary Buddhist principles are to treat others with respect and loving kindness and to do others no harm, psychologically or physically. If you keep that in mind, you will see that the Theravadan monk's answer was not really apposite ... one can have two consenting adults and still have a total lack of respect and loving kindness, and the likelihood of psychological harm from casual sex is not to be minimized. Indeed, even in a marriage, it is quite possible for the foundations of "skillful" (and I obviously don't mean technique here) sex to be missing and that therefore even in that setting sex could be misconduct using the standard I have noted.[34]

The fourth Precept states, "Aware of the suffering caused by unmindful speech and the inability to listen to others, I am committed to cultivating loving speech and deep listening in order to bring joy and happiness to others and relieve others of their suffering. Knowing that words can create happiness or suffering, I am determined to speak truthfully, with words that inspire self-confidence, joy, and hope." While this precept seems rather innocuous and people rarely react to it quizzically, as they do with the third

---

[34] For a fuller discussion of this issue, see the section,"Sex," in my book, *Making Your Way in Life as a Buddhist.*

Precept, it is a very difficult precept for most of us to practice.

First, let's look at deep listening. What does "deep listening" mean? It means to really hear what the other person is saying. For one to practice deep listening, one must therefore listen free of ones own ego. Otherwise you are hearing what is said through the filter of your own perception and biases and thus not really hearing what the other person is saying, where that person is coming from. Thus when someone says, "I hear you," they rarely do.

So if you are not yet free of your ego, how then do you practice this Precept, how do you listen deeply? It's almost impossible. The best you can do is be aware how your ego is filtering and reacting to what is being said and try to put that aside. From personal experience I can say that it is possible to catch that you are reacting to something through your ego and to very consciously put that to one side and reabsorb what is being said. For example, often when someone is voicing their feelings about something, especially something personal, all they want is to be listened to; they are not looking to get into a discussion. Yet our ego wants to have a chance to comment, to have input, to feel good about helping the person … but that is not helping the person. At some point, and this was not at all easy, I learned to sit quietly and just listen.

What does it mean to "speak with loving kindness." It means more than just being kind to the other person. It means speaking out of unconditional love for the person and to speak selflessly. As with listening deeply, this requires one to be free of ego, and if not, to catch yourself as your ego starts to form thoughts and words in your mind. And it requires your heart to be open to the person regardless of what they have done or what they may do, including whether they listen to what you have to say and act as you suggest. Indeed, speaking with loving kindness may mean not speaking at all, as previously noted.

The fifth Precept is again one that is very challenging living in out culture. The precept states, "Aware of the suffering caused by unmindful consumption, I am committed to cultivating good health, both physical and mental, for myself, my family, and my society by practicing mindful eating, drinking, and consuming. I will ingest only items that preserve peace, well being, and joy in my body, in my consciousness, and in the collective body and consciousness of my family and society."

The reason why this is challenging is that our culture promotes unmindful consumption and our economy is premised on it. You may think that you are consuming mindfully ... whether it's things you purchase, or what you read, or what you watch on television or in the movies ... but consuming mindfully means more than making a conscious decision. It means being sufficiently aware that you are mindful of why you are thinking about consuming something and you are aware of the impact of such consuming on you and thus have the ability to decide not to consume the thing in those instances where you understand that consuming it will not "preserve peace, wellbeing, and joy."

This precept, although Thich Nhat Hanh frames it with reference to the broader community, is the precept that most concerns refraining from doing harm to oneself, of not doing things that add to or feed our samsara. And again, since this is not "harm" as our culture defines the word, but spiritual "harm," practicing this precept requires not just discipline, but a 24/7 practice of mindfulness.

By purposefully practicing the Five Precepts, your mindfulness will increase, which is essential if you are eventually to surrender your ego to your true Buddha nature. If you are serious about following the Buddhist path but have not yet formally "taken" the Precepts, I would encourage you to do so if you attend a temple or there is one is reasonable proximity to where you live. It is a step on the path, a commitment of oneself, which is essential to gaining greater understanding.

UNDERSTANDING

The third Paramita is often referred to as patience or acceptance. Other terms used are forbearance and tolerance. While these terms are all applicable, they do not get at the essence of this Paramita, which is the capacity to face adversity, insult, distress, and the wrongs of others not just without resentment, irritation or retaliation … it is the capacity to practice compassion even towards someone or a group of people who is acting wrongfully towards you. The quality that better defines this capacity is, I think, "understanding," which encompasses all the others.

This Paramita goes beyond saying, "It's just the way it is." It is more than acceptance and more than patience. It's more than forbearance and tolerance. It's an embracing of the sometime-hostile world out there and a compassion based on unconditional love for everyone that is part of it.

How does one practice this Paramita? How does one get to the point where one is able to react in this manner to adversity?

The key is remembering that everyone on this earth, regardless of his or her status in life, suffers from samsara. And that the learned experience that forms their ego and creates their samsara makes each person who he is. We may all be born essentially perfect with the true Buddha nature inside us, and have that commonality, but the other commonality is that we all suffer and are prisoners of our ego.

And because each of us was born in different circumstances and has had different life experiences, we grow up differently and become different people. Regardless what we become … whether a Nazi SS guard or a Buddhist monk, to take two extremes … it's a function of our learned experience. Always remember the saying, "There but for good fortune, or the grace of God, go I."

When you come to truly understand this truth, then you will have compassion for those that harm you and others, for you will be aware of their samsara, of the terrible suffering that they experience, and you will know that their range of free will is very narrow, bounded as it is by their learned experience. When someone insults you or harms you, you will not take it personally because it is a kind of programmed robot that does these things, not the true person that, just as with you, is the true Buddha nature.[35]

Without question this way of reacting to adversity is contrary to everything that we've learned. It goes against the very fiber of our being, that is to say our ego. So arriving at this state of understanding will require disciplined meditation and awareness.

As with most things on the Buddhist path, this understanding will most likely not come quickly, and it will come in increments rather than all at once. If you are like most people, you will find that the less egregious the adversity, the more quickly you will be able to react with understanding. As you make the effort to practice this Paramita, do not forget to have compassion for yourself regarding the difficulty of "perfecting" the Paramita of understanding.

---

[35] This does not mean that people are not responsible for their acts. They are. But it does impact concepts of punishment and rehabilitation. How this squares with a criminal justice system based on the concept of free will is beyond the scope of this writing. But for an extensive discussion of this subject see, David Eagleman, "The Brain on Trial," *The Atlantic*, July/August 2011

ENTHUSIASTIC EFFORT AND DILIGENCE

Because the culture we live in and our ego place obstacles in our path every day, following the path, staying on it, is not easy. Practicing the fourth Paramita of enthusiastic effort and diligence provides us with the energy, courage, and endurance to stay our course and not be led astray.

To practice this Paramita requires unequivocal faith in the Buddha dharma. Only with such faith and the joy that comes from that faith can one have the stamina to withstand the almost withering assault your ego will wage daily against your efforts to follow the path.

The other source of strength, in addition to the Buddha and the Buddha dharma, is the sangha. Living in a world and in a culture that is so inhospitable to the Buddhist path, it is more than helpful, I would say necessary, to be in touch with other Buddhists. Whether it's through a local temple you attend, or online interaction, or even reading the writings of other contemporary Buddhists, the support provided through such activities makes a big difference in your ability to joyfully persevere in the discipline of your practice.

The essence of what I'm saying here is that found in the "Three Jewels" mantra:

"I take refuge in Buddha.
I take refuge in Dharma.
I take refuge in Sangha."

There is nothing more central to following the Buddhist path.

MEDITATION/CONCENTRATION

Although this is the fifth Paramita, it is the lynchpin on which the perfection of the other Paramitas and our progress on the Buddhist path rests. As the poem, *Master Hakuin's Chant in Praise of Zazen*, says, "The cause of our sorrow is ego delusion. From dark path to dark path we've wandered in darkness. How can we be free of birth and death? The gateway to freedom is zazen samadhi, beyond exaltation, beyond all our praises, the pure Mahajana.[36]

There is no progress on the Buddhist path without a disciplined, daily meditation practice. Because without regular meditation, there is no hope of finding clarity regarding yourself and the world around you. Without the concentration, focus, and quiet of meditation, there is no hope of hearing the voice of your own true Buddha nature above the din of the messages of our culture and voice of your ego and of finding equanimity.

But the fifth Paramita is about more than your formal meditation practice, the time you spend sitting on your cushion or doing walking meditation. It's about having the concentration to be mindful throughout the day. The practice of observing mindfully, of seeing things without the intervention of thought, of being present throughout the day has been discussed earlier in this book. Without being present and mindful throughout the day one cannot implement whatever clarity you found during your meditation because your mind will be overwhelmed with the noise of the surrounding culture and voice of your ego.

And without that practical application, you will actually increase your suffering because on the one hand you now have an awareness of what is going on in your interaction with yourself and the world around you, and yet you will not feel able to make any changes. This can be a very

---

[36] Roshi Philip Kapleau, op. cit.

painful and frustrating part of the path. You may well throw down your books and curse the day you opened your mind to the Buddha dharma.

If you are at this point, practicing the Paramita of meditation/concentration and practicing the Paramita of enthusiastic effort and diligence is of great importance. Never lose faith that if you follow the path and practice the six Paramitas that you will come to a point where your entire life and being will be suffused with peace, contentment, and happiness.

At first you will need to be mindful and make practical application of the teachings purposefully by stopping and centering yourself using one of the techniques suggested earlier in the book. But as time passes, and your practice deepens, you will find that you have more and longer periods of mindfulness during the day without purposefully stopping. You will have learned to listen for the voice of your true Buddha nature at all times.

WISDOM

Wisdom here does not mean the knowledge that comes from reading books or studying. Wisdom here is an intuitive state. It is beyond all thought. It is beyond acceptance and rejection, hope and fear ... it is beyond all labels. It is a place where, as stated in the ancient Chinese poem, *Affirming Faith in Mind,* "All's self-revealing, void and clear, without exerting power of mind. Thought cannot reach this state of truth, here feelings are of no avail."[37]

How does one ever attain or perfect this wisdom? Actually, since this wisdom is the essence of our true Buddha nature, it is already in us, we don't have to attain it. What we do need to do is find it, uncover it, let it breathe the fresh air of life.

And how we do that is by following all the steps discussed in this book, including those covered in the next and last chapter, "Surrendering the Ego and Finding Freedom."

Over the years, one of the most compelling chants I recited at temple was the Heart Sutra ... The Heart of Perfected Wisdom. If you are not yet familiar with it, it is, with its contemplation on emptiness and the process of spiritual development that leads to enlightenment, a central sutra of the Buddhist Mahayana tradition. It is the essence of the sixth Paramita. Its core truths are the key to freeing ourselves and it is typically chanted on a regular basis.

But after years of chanting the sutra in various translations, I had the feeling as my practice deepened that the translations were inadequate. Some suffered from a use of English that lacked clarity or just seemed wrong. And all seemed to me to be missing something important in the first verse.

---

[37] ibid.

In that verse, these versions uniformly stated that when the Bodhisattva Avelokiteshvara perceived that all five skandhas were empty of intrinsic existence his suffering ceased. The causal connection is direct. So, for example, in the lovely translation by Roshi Philip Kapleau:

> *"saw the emptiness of all five skandhas and sundered the bonds that create suffering."*[38]

It seemed to me that as a teaching tool, which the sutras are, the concept of the oneness of all things, of experiencing things without the intervention of thought, was missing as a bridge from realizing the emptiness of the skandhas to being free of suffering. I know how presumptuous this must sound, but I felt it in my gut.

Having been a onetime student of language, I knew the problems and misunderstandings that can result depending on how words are translated. After not being able to find a monk who was interested in working on this project with me, I decided to give it a go myself.

I chose to base my translation on the Chinese text and so gathered several Chinese editions of the sutra. In comparing them, I found that they all were identical and so felt safe proceeding with the project. Armed with several Chinese dictionaries I tackled the translation.

As I worked through the first verse, I found what I had thought had to be there. Between the phrase positing the perception of the emptiness of the skandhas and that regarding the cessation of suffering was the phrase "度一", literally "passing through one." Taking the liberties in translation (and exposition) that are not uncommon in these texts to clarify meaning, I translated this phrase:

---

[38] ibid.

"Thus being at one with all things,
Experiencing things directly without the intervention of thought"

What follows is my translation of the Heart Sutra.[39]

---

[39] I should note that in the process of working on this project, I found that in the Sanskrit text, and the Tibetan text derived from the Sanskrit, the first verse ends with perceiving the emptiness of the skandhas; there is no mention of suffering ceasing. The Chinese translation dates from around 400 A.D. and was done by a well-known Indian scholar and Buddhist missionary. I have found no explanation for this apparent variance. Since the Heart Sutra is not a sutra that was delivered by the Buddha, it would seem that one could use either version, depending on ones Buddhist lineage.

PRACTICING THE SIX PARAMITAS

    Prajna Paramita Hridaya – Heart of Perfected Wisdom

The Bodhisattva Avelokiteshvara,
Practicing the perfection of wisdom, going deep within,
Was illuminated and perceived that
All five skandhas are empty of intrinsic existence.
Thus being at one with all things,
Experiencing things directly without the intervention of
    thought,
All suffering and doubt ceased.

Shariputra, the appearance of form is not separate from
    emptiness,
Emptiness is not separate from the appearance of form,
The appearance of form is one with emptiness,
Emptiness is one with appearance of form.
The same is true for feelings, perceptions, mental
    formations, and consciousness-ego.

Shariputra, all dharmas – all appearance of phenomena – are
    mutually empty:
There is neither birth nor death,
Neither defilement nor purity,
Neither gain nor loss.

Therefore, within emptiness there is no appearance of form
No feelings, perceptions, mental formations, or
    consciousness-ego,
No eye, ear, nose, tongue, body, thought,
No color, sound, smell, taste, touch, or the appearance of
    phenomena,
Not even the domain of sight
Nor the domain of consciousness-ego.

No ignorance or end of ignorance,
Nor aging and death or end of them,

No creation of suffering or noble path to end suffering.
No wisdom nor its attainment,
There is nothing to attain.

Bodhisattvas, abiding always in perfected wisdom,
Their minds have no fears or obstructions,
Therefore they have no fears or obstructions;
Free of confused illusions,
They reach nirvana.

All Buddhas of past, present, and future time,
Abiding always in perfected wisdom
Come to full enlightenment.

Therefore let all know that perfected wisdom
Is the most spiritual mantra,
The most radiant mantra.
None is higher than it
Nor equal to it,
It is able to relieve all suffering,
It is the essence of truth, not false.

Therefore, say the mantra of perfected wisdom:
Gate gate,
Paragate,
Parasamgate,
Bodhi svaha

For me, the power of this sutra is that it does not describe what it is like to be enlightened, but rather it shows the path, or markers on the path, to enlightenment. Boddhisatvas after all are not yet enlightened beings ... the Buddha himself referred to his pre-enlightened state as a Boddhisatva.[40]

---

[40] B. Nanamoli, op.cit., p.10

There are several sections of the sutra that are especially edifying and became more so for me through my translation work. The first verse states in just a few scant words the essence of Buddhist teaching ... that all our perceptions are illusory, without inherent existence, and that when we realize this we are able to be one with all things (having surrendered our ego to our true Buddha nature). All barriers are gone, and we experience and observe things without the intervention of thought.[41] It is this freedom from thought that ends our doubt and suffering.

As a later verse reiterates, when you reach this state "your mind has no fears or obstructions, therefore you have no fears or obstructions. Free of confused illusions, you reach nirvana." You have freed yourself from the known.

The point is that our lives are ruled by the labels our learned experience places on everything we encounter in life and that when one reaches the stage of ones practice that is the perfection of wisdom, one is free of these labels and their resulting obstructions.

The verses that list examples of this truth are powerful indeed. "There is neither birth nor death." This seemingly clear statement gives many people pause at first. But the sutra here does not contradict this central fact of life or the Buddha's teaching ... that all things that arise eventually fall ... rather it means that our thoughts about birth and death, our perception of those two states, are illusory. And when we realize that the five skandhas are empty of intrinsic existence, those perceptions fall away. The labels, the way we think of birth and death are no more. And so the fear we have of death based on those labels is no more.

The same is true of "neither defilement or purity." Many people reading the sutra for the first time again just

---

[41] Again to be clear. as noted in an earlier footnote, thought and the aggregates are always present, even the Buddha had feelings, perceptions, and thoughts, but by not attaching to our thoughts, they do not intervene in our experience of things.

shake their heads in bewilderment. "How can there be no such thing as defilement?"

But here too, the sutra is not saying that the acts that we label as defilement don't happen ... bad things happen to many innocent people ... but that the interpretation of these acts as a defilement of the person have no intrinsic nature. One is defiled only because our culture or learned experience says you are defiled. Whereas if you know that your true Buddha nature is totally unaffected by what has happened, then you are not defiled and the experience of the act does not cause mental suffering.

"Ok," you may say, "but what about the line that says, 'No creation of suffering or noble path to end suffering.' That's what the Four Noble Truths, the most central of the Buddha's teachings, is all about. It makes no sense."

Again, you have to consider the context. The sutra is talking about one who perceives the emptiness of all five skandhas and thus is free of doubt and suffering. Well, if you are at that stage of your practice, then there is no creation of suffering or noble path to end suffering. Suffering for such individuals does not exist.

This is the promise of the Buddhist path, and it is not just available to the enlightened. As I state at other places in this book, for most of us the experience of the Buddhist path is incremental. We do not become enlightened in a flash. Indeed, we may never reach full enlightenment, always remaining at some stage just short of it. But as we progress on the path, we experience more and more the freedom from thought that is described in the sutra and the peace that comes with it.

Chapter 6
Surrendering the Ego and Finding Freedom

1.

> "The cause of our sorrow is ego delusion.
> From dark path to dark path
> We've wandered in darkness.
> How can we be free from birth and death?
> The gateway to freedom is zazen samadhi,
> Beyond all our praises, beyond exaltation,
> The pure Mahayana."[42]

....

And so after years of practice, following the steps that I have outlined in the previous chapters, I had found much peace and happiness. On the issues that were not central to my ego, to the samsara that roiled in my gut, I was able to reasonably consistently follow the path, living a life in keeping with the Five Precepts, accepting myself and my life as it is, and being at one with things, observing them without the intervention of thought. I was acutely aware of the emptiness of all thought.

But as to those issues that were at the core of my suffering, I was not much further on the path than when I started. I had chipped away at the edges of my ego, but that's all. I was not able to be aware of such thoughts rising. There was no acceptance, no nonattachment, no oneness

---

[42] Roshis Philip Kapleau, op. cit.

with those parts of me. My ego coexisted actively with my otherwise increased state of mindfulness.

Then one day during a dharma talk, Huyen Te said to us that we had come far but we were still standing on the precipice. We were not able to jump because our ego was still in control and we feared an ego-free unknown. He said that the choice was ours, we had only to surrender our ego to our true Buddha nature. It was as straight forward as that.

This was true. I felt it in my gut. And I knew without any doubt that as the poem says, "the cause of my suffering is ego delusion." Yet even after years of practice, I could not take that step of surrendering my ego, jumping off the precipice. I acknowledged that the present paradigms that directed my life were to a large extent harmful and yet my fear of the unknown prevented me from taking that step.

And while I was familiar with the concept of surrendering ones ego from my 12-step work, and probably because of that familiarity, Huyen Te's suggestion that "that's all we had to do" was greeted by me with a resounding, "Ha!". It sounds so straightforward and simple, yet I knew it would be anything but.

But I had faith in Huyen Te's teaching and knew in my heart that the path he had shown us was the answer, and so after some procrastination and pushing back, I committed myself to that path. From my past experience, I knew that commitment and faith were key to making progress. I had to proceed with no more doubt or fear. And with great patience and discipline.

Over the course of the next four years my practice continued to deepen, supported by my experiences at the temple, not just from the teaching I received but by the good fellowship of the other members of the sangha. In Buddhism we take refuge in the three jewels ... the Buddha, the Dharma, and the Sangha. Without question, the warmth and community that was our sangha was a wonderful weekly experience for me.

And yet I cannot say that I made much if any progress on surrendering my ego with respect to my core issues. Nor should this be surprising. We are talking here of psychological issues that formed during childhood and became central defining elements of my perspective regarding myself, of my ego. If the cultural habit-energies of decades are hard to free oneself from, freeing ourselves from the definition of who we are is even harder

Two things happened during this period of time that were significant in moving me along my path and further loosening the chains of the past.

I had been trying for some time while meditating to somehow connect with my true Buddha nature, to visualize this non-physical thing, to no avail. Then one day as I was meditating I suddenly saw before me smiling, laughing images of me as a young toddler. I knew immediately that there was my true Buddha nature, taking joy in the moment for no particular reason, full of love, an innocent in the world unburdened by learned experience ... and I cried deeply and long. Not uncoincidently I'm sure, my mother had within the previous few months sent me both my baby book and an album of photos of me as a baby and toddler!

Then one day, a year or so after that, while in the process of going through my files to clean them out, I came upon two loving letters from my father that I had totally forgotten about. One was a letter he wrote to me in 1985 on my 41st birthday. The other was a copy of a letter that my father had written in 1956 just before he was to undergo an operation, and which my mother had sent me in 1993, four years after his death. I mention this episode because the feelings I developed as a child of not being loved by my father and of his feeling I wasn't normal were central causes of my samsara.

After reading these letters, I broke down and sobbed uncontrollably for some time. Here was tangible proof of the love that I had always sought to be reassured of. And

87

yet I realized that I had been so wound up in my hurt and the perception of not being loved, so committed to distancing myself emotionally from my father through all those years, that when I had originally received those two letters they did not make a dent in that perception, and the letters went unremembered until I went through my files that day. I had been that closed to his love. What a loss.

I had always been aware of the profound positive impact that my father had had on my character, but that awareness and gratitude didn't translate into deep warmth and affection; it didn't cross the barrier I had erected. Now, reading here his eloquent expression of his love and respect for me and who he was as a person, what he believed in, and what he wanted in life, I was overwhelmed with feelings of love and, again, loss.

Here was a clear example of how perceptions that we may develop as a child, while totally understandable, are nevertheless false. And it was an example of how these learned experiences have such a hold on our psyche that we cannot shake ourselves free, even after years of following the path and being fully aware of the illusory nature of our perceptions

Yet my ego remained untouched by these cathartic experiences. Obviously, neither intellectual thought and understanding nor even emotional cathartic experiences were enough to free me from the chains of my past. Just as obviously, my disciplined meditation practice, while it had brought my practice far and enabled me to experience much peace and happiness in many areas of my life, had not enabled me to free myself from my ego on these core issues. Where to turn?

2.

As the Buddha said, "But to be rid of the conceit 'I am' – that is the greatest happiness of all." I thought I knew so much and had come so far, but that was part of the problem. It was only when I humbly went back to basics that I reconnected with the light of my true Buddha mind and discovered my oneness with all things.

. . . .

Fast-forward several years. In March of 2007, a Buddhist acquaintance told me that *Tricycle Magazine* (a magazine about Buddhism) was promoting a 28-day at-home retreat. He was going to do it and he wondered whether I would be interested; we could support each other in this effort.

When I checked out the details in the magazine, my initial reaction was that this retreat really wouldn't help me, that my practice was already quite disciplined in the sense that I practiced daily. But then I thought about it more carefully and realized that the retreat would actually add various levels of discipline to my daily practice and that it might indeed be helpful.

For I had been standing at a crossroad for a long time ... despite my commitment to jump off the precipice, I *still* had not been able to surrender my ego to my true Buddha nature. Yes, I was still stuck in the same place despite the teaching of Huyen Te and Thai Tue. My practice had continued to deepen, my awareness had increased, I observed most things without the intervention of thought, but there remained a barrier, certainly as to my core issues ... I was still not one with my true Buddha nature. And so I decided to do the retreat.

My daily practice for years had consisted of a walking and sitting meditation in the morning, about 15 and 30 minutes respectively, shortly after I got up. But often the meditation was not disciplined, as I would fall into focused thought on some current issue of mine. I sat quietly, yes, but my thought was engaged; I was not an observer.

The retreat took me back to the basics. The first week, there was a 30-minute morning and evening sitting meditation; during the rest of the day I carried on with my normal daily activities. During the meditations, I observed only my breath and the sounds around me; my mind was silent except for the occasional random thought that passed through (what Huyen Te referred to as "our unfinished business") but to which I did not attach.

Already after the first week, I felt a deepening of my practice and an increase in calm and peace. The second week was basically the same, with a walking meditation added during the day.

The third week, the morning and evening sitting meditation periods were increased to 45 minutes. This was a good stretch for me because it required me to deal with the restlessness and physical discomfort that often comes when sitting for longer periods of time. I would recognize those feelings or sensations, greet them, and then let them go.

During the fourth week, I decided to use part of my sitting meditation time to concentrate on various basic tenets of Buddhism so as to gain a deeper understanding. One day I also focused on loneliness. These were not focused meditations in the sense of my previous daily meditation practice where I was actively engaged in thought. Instead, I just put a concept out there and without thinking let my mind explore its essence.

The final day of the retreat was a total silent retreat from sunrise to sunset. I did four or five 45-minute sitting meditations and several walking meditations. During the rest of the day I either read Buddhist literature or sat silently.

One of the books I read that final retreat day was a section of Sogyal Rinpoche's *Tibetan Book of Living and Dying*[43] that I hadn't read previously. This was my first exposure to the Tibetan practice of "tonglen," giving and receiving ... taking on the suffering and pain of others and giving them your happiness, well-being, and peace of mind.

Sogyal Rinpoche recommends starting this practice by first doing it for yourself. Before one can have such compassion for others, one has to have compassion for oneself. The first step is to *"unseal the spring of loving kindness."* To do that he suggests going back in your mind and recreate, almost visualize, a love that someone gave you that really moved you. My mind wandered through several possibilities both in my adult life and childhood, when suddenly I remembered an instance with my father that was repeated often when I was small ... he would come to my bed at night when he would get home and play with my toes.

When I remembered that episode, which had long since been forgotten, I cried because of the love that I was feeling from my father and almost simultaneously a big smile formed on my face. Rinpoche says that, *"You will remember then that even though you may not always feel that you have been loved enough, you were loved genuinely once. Knowing that now will make you feel again that you are, as that person made you feel then, worthy of love and really lovable."* And so it did.

Under his further instruction, I let my heart open and the love that flowed from it was extended to my father, to my family and friends, and to all people. I visualized holding my father as he was dying (I was not there in fact) and saying to him, "You can let go now for I know that you love me and I love you ... I will be ok." I was now ready to practice tonglen on myself.

---

[43] Sogyal Rinpoche, op. cit.

Rinpoche suggests, for the purpose of this exercise, dividing yourself into two aspects ... one is the aspect of you that is whole, compassionate, etc., the other is the aspect of you that has been hurt, that feels misunderstood, bitter or angry, *"who might have been unjustly treated or abused as a child, or has suffered in relationships or been wronged by society."* As you breathe in, the first aspect opens its heart completely and receives all of the other aspect's pain and suffering. As you breathe out, the first aspect gives the other aspect all its healing love, warmth, trust, and happiness. In response, the other aspect opens its heart to this love and all pain and suffering melt away in this embrace.

What could be more appropriate for me given my history, I thought! And so, I practiced tonglen on myself with beneficial results. Indeed, as the weeks and months passed after the retreat, I practiced both the visualization of my father's love, as well as tonglen on myself, on a regular basis. Each time I did, I felt that smile ... the smile of happiness and love ... form naturally and for many weeks tears would roll down my cheek. Clearly, this was a very cathartic experience for me.

The last breakthrough, which probably built on these exercises I had done, came when I was reading the Heart Sutra. I suddenly realized that I had been reading the language about being at one with all things and experiencing things directly without the intervention of thought as applying solely to things outside of my self.

While I had for a long time been aware of the illusory nature of all my perceptions and feelings about my self, I had never applied the teaching of the Heart Sutra to my self ... I had not been at one with my self and did not experience my self without the intervention of thought. I had surrendered my ego to my true Buddha nature on every subject other than my self. I knew at that instant that that was why despite all my progress, my core suffering had continued.

What a shock. Let me clarify. I had known that I wasn't at one with my true Buddha nature, else why would I still be suffering. But I hadn't understood why. The realization that I had come to be at one with most things but not with my own self and that I hadn't even realized my restricted reading of the Heart Sutra was painful.

After this realization, I immediately meditated on being at one with my self, my true Buddha nature, and experiencing my self without the intervention of thought. It was another cathartic experience and I cried.

The result of this final week and final day of my at-home retreat was that, for the first time, I knew that *all* things are impermanent and that *all* perceptions are illusory ... not just intellectually but at the core of my being. I surrendered *all* aspects of my ego to my true Buddha nature and was at one with myself and all things. When I read various Buddhist texts on the final day, texts that I had read and underlined many times before, I read them with a deep understanding that I had never had before. And I was at least for that moment, that day, free at last of loneliness and rejection because I knew those labels for what they were ... just labels that were products of my mind, not reflections of reality. I was free of my ego.

I could tell in the following days that I was interacting with things and people ... whether it was panhandlers on the street, homeless people in the park, or thinking about the people who slaughtered their neighbors and strangers in Rwanda ... on a different level, in a different way. I thought before that I had compassion for all people and was at one with them, but that was an ego deception. Now I truly understood my oneness with them and felt great compassion for them as human beings rather than fear and revulsion or pity. I was aware of their suffering, that we are all products of our environment.

SURRENDERING THE EGO AND FINDING FREEDOM

Who am I?

I am the tree I see,
The flower that blooms,
The morning rain,
And the cold night air.

I am the bird in flight,
The wounded bear,
The howling wolf,
And the dog lying before the fire.

I am the laughing child,
The old lady begging,
The dope addict,
And the forgetful old man.

I am all things,
And I am nothing

Written on the final day of my at-home retreat, April 14, 2007

3.

It is now several years after my at-home retreat. I know that my ego is still part of me, just waiting for a moment of weakness to arise, but that's ok ... I am aware, most of the time. And when it arises I "speak" to it, telling it that I am free of all unskillful desires and that it has no more power over my life. And then it reluctantly subsides.

I realized recently that there was something at work during my at-home retreat that I was not aware of at the time. The reason why the retreat had such an impact was that by going deeper into my meditation and immersing myself totally in my spirituality on the final day, I had not just surrendered my ego, I had turned my will and my life over to my true Buddha nature. I was at last one with my true Buddha mind.

A friend had recently shared with me a thought he had while meditating. He said that there's no way to sort through all the issues that come up in his mind; his ego-mind won't allow him any consistent clarity. And so he said he decided that he needed to take a back seat in the process of his spiritual development and let Arjuna (he's reading a Hindu text) take care of things.

When his words came to me while I was meditating the next morning, I realized something that had been missing from my writing. What my friend was doing is a core step in all 12-step programs ... turning your will and your life over to your higher power, realizing that only it can bring you peace. Your higher power can be your true Buddha nature, or Arjuna, as in his case, or whatever. The point is that there is a spiritual power within us that can lead us out of samsara if we only allow it to.

In the teaching I've received and my writings, the ultimate key has been to surrender your ego to your true Buddha nature. As stated, that is a very willful act. And as I know from my 12-step program background, addiction is self-will run riot. I've written earlier in this book that our cravings are basically addictions. And so, for example, in order to give acceptance a chance to take root, we need to do what is taught in 12-step programs and forego all desires until we can say that we truly accept our lives and ourselves as we are. Only then can we have skillful desires.

And so the wisdom of 12-step programs needs to be incorporated in the Fourfold Path to Freedom as well. The fourth step of the Fourfold Path thus becomes, *"Surrendering our ego to our true Buddha nature, turning our will and our lives over to our true Buddha nature."* When we surrender our ego to our true Buddha nature, what we are doing is taking a back seat and putting our will and our lives in the hands of our true Buddha nature. That still is an act of will and our ego will still fight mightily against it, but it is far less willful than pure surrender.

Perhaps of even greater impact, surrendering your ego is a scary concept. As I related earlier, the monk from whom I received this teaching said after we were working on this for a while that while we had come far, we were still standing on the precipice. We had not jumped off it into the land of nirvana because we were scared of the unknown. And how right he was.

By incorporating the concept of turning our will and our lives over to our true Buddha nature, it turns the surrender of our ego into a warm and comforting act for we know we have nothing to fear from putting our lives in the hands of our true Buddha nature. This may all seem like semantics, a distinction without a difference, but the words we speak or think, the approach we take, can make a significant difference in our overcoming the barriers to making further progress on the path.

It took me years of practice after receiving this teaching on surrender to actually be able to surrender my ego to my true Buddha nature. Perhaps the reason why it took so long, besides the craftiness and strength of my ego-mind, was both that I was approaching this as a willful act as opposed to just turning my will over to my true Buddha nature and that the concept of surrender and jumping off the precipice was scary. Without any question in my mind, combining these two thoughts as I have now suggested is an improved teaching.

What also makes it a more powerful teaching is that it not only explicitly acknowledges ones belief that your true Buddha nature exists but that only it can bring you peace. I have written earlier in this book that belief in the teachings of the Buddha is the cornerstone on which all progress on the path rests. Without that belief there is nothing.

I also realized recently I had one more barrier to cross. The classic Chinese poem "Affirming Faith in Mind" says:

In this true world of Emptiness
both self and other are no more.
To enter this true empty world,
immediately affirm "not-two."
In this "not-two" all is the same,
with nothing separate or outside.[44]

After a lifetime of feeling separate from most others, I had thought that with the compassion I now had for all people and things, being usually self-less in my actions, feeling at one with all things in the sense that we are all in this boat of the world together and have the commonality of our samsara and our true Buddha natures, and experiencing things for the most part directly without the intervention of thought having surrendered my ego to my true Buddha nature, that I had crossed the barrier of "not-two," which limits further progress on the path.

But recently when a friend was talking about feeling that he doesn't belong anywhere, I thought about my own

---

[44] ibid.

experiences past and present. And I realized that while I do feel that in coming and going I never leave home ... I carry my home with me wherever I am because my home, my refuge, is the Buddha, my faith in his teachings, and my meditation practice ... I nevertheless felt separate from my surroundings; I felt I did not belong. I may have felt at one with all things, and yet in this sense I felt separate. I could not say "not-two."

My initial reaction was that with all one reads in the news each day about the extent of hatred and evil in the world, and the past social rejections and hurt I had myself experienced, it would be hard to feel "not-two" even while having compassion for those who have such feelings or commit such acts and loving them unconditionally. I said to myself that this feeling of self and other does not come from thought, it comes from a direct awareness of the facts of life. Even regarding my personal life, I knew what was illusion and what was real. Nevertheless this feeling of separateness, which I had not been so acutely aware of for some time, unsettled me.

Then one morning, something I had recently re-read in Krishnamurti[45] came to mind ... "fear is thought." And I suddenly realized that I had taken those directly experienced facts and turned them into thoughts, and the thoughts created fear. But it was at such a low level of intensity that I wasn't even aware of it until my friend made that statement which caused me to reflect on my own feelings about my surroundings. There is still so much to be learned ... or better put, to be mindful of.

This fear had held me back from interaction with others, strangers, for most of my life (with the one definite exception being the period immediately after my at-home retreat just discussed). Now that I had discerned that and meditated on it, I felt free of that fear and was able to relate

---

[45] J. Krishnamurti, op. cit.

to my surroundings and people without that barrier. What a gift!

It has been almost two years since I began writing on Buddhism and it has been a journey that I am grateful for. I know that I can never be the care-free person that smiles at me from those photos of me as a toddler for I have observed and learned too much about the world. But I have rediscovered the unconditional love for myself and the unconditional love and compassion for those around me and indeed for all sentient beings that that child ... the embodiment of my true Buddha nature ... felt. And for the most part I observe and experience myself and the world without the intervention of thought. I have returned to my self-nature.

This is not to say that my ego never arises and that when it does, I always catch it and respond to it appropriately. For example, sometimes I say something in conversation and only realize later that that was my ego talking; if I had been mindful, I would have been silent or said something else. I was neither listening deeply or speaking with loving kindness.

Life continues to be a challenge, not so much in interacting with myself but in interacting or reacting to all the troubling things that happen around me, whether closer at hand or in the broader world. But I meet that challenge now with a calmness and a perspective that does not arouse my passions. I am able to see things clearly.

I don't know at this point where all of this will lead. And I'm not really concerned about that. I feel strongly that if I live each day well, the future will take care of itself. I live a good and full life today in the present. What more can one ask for?

www.ingramcontent.com/pod-product-compliance
Lightning Source LLC
Chambersburg PA
CBHW051658040426
42446CB00009B/1193